WIN TRUE

How you win matters
on and off the bike

Scott Mercier
and Laurena Mayne Davis

ISBN: 9798409119546

MORE PRAISE FOR *WIN TRUE*

"In my more than forty years of coaching, Scott Mercier was one of the most talented and determined athletes I worked with. His path from Category 4 racer to Olympian and then professional cyclist was full of highs and lows, and in *Win True* he gives readers a front row seat to the good, bad, and ugly of elite-level cycling."
—Chris Carmichael, Founder of Carmichael Training Systems (CTS)

"Scott Mercier shares his experiences of riding elbow-to-elbow with the best cyclists in the world — while competing as a clean rider — during one of the darkest periods in the sport's history. His is a riveting account of racing in Europe's Classics and the Barcelona Olympics while illuminating the pressures and temptations a young cyclist was faced with in the quest to earn a living and be competitive in this secret, compromised world."
—Neal Beidleman, mountaineer and engineer

"Win True is a classic. Character is the most important element of effective leadership and is the foundation for everything we do in life. Scott Mercier proved that in a very painful but honorable way. At West Point we teach our cadets to choose the 'harder right over the easier wrong,' and Scott's life exemplifies that truth in this incredible book."
—Lt. General Robert L. Caslen Jr. (retired), author of *The Character Edge*

"In a world desperate for modern-day profiles in courage, Scott Mercier's story fits the bill. To walk away from a sport he loved based upon his moral standards is inspiring. As I have connected Scott with groups of students and college athletes across multiple sports to share his story, I have seen countless 'light bulb moments' first hand. This book is a must-read for young people engaged in competitive sports and, really, anyone hoping for a life guided by integrity in the pursuit of meaning."

—Tim Foster, former President of Colorado Mesa University

"Scott Mercier is a champion in every sense of the word. Whether he was competing at the pinnacle of global cycling or in the business world, Scott has been steadfast to his principles. His story is fascinating, and his example of leadership and integrity is one to which we all aspire."

—Tom Clancy, Chief Investment Officer for the State of Pennsylvania

This book is dedicated to my wife, Mandie,
who gave up everything for me.

Win True

PROLOGUE

I grabbed the brass ring when I signed with the U.S. Postal Service Professional Cycling Team for the 1997 season. Check that: Postal was next level, and that ring wasn't brass, it was golden.

I'd fought my way through the amateur, the Olympic, and the professional ranks, but Postal was where I yearned to race. It was a moneyed team. A team that competed among the elite in Europe. A team as ambitious as I was.

As a new Postal rider, there were some familiar training regimes, but there were some new temptations, too.

I'd heard the rumors of pervasive doping in the elite races in Europe, but I hadn't been directly confronted with it racing in America. We had a few riders who doped for preternatural advantage, like in many sports, but it wasn't widespread. It wasn't programmatic.

It wasn't the first thing out of your new team doctor's mouth.

The Postal training camp was in Alpine, California, in the coastal mountains outside San Diego. It was there that I met our team doctor, a friendly Spaniard named Pedro Celaya. He started with a blood test on each rider to begin a blood profile. Pedro checked riders' blood values for a variety of things, but what he really wanted to see was our hematocrit levels, which showed the percentage of oxygen-carrying red blood cells. I scored a low 40.5 percent.

When Pedro read my values he frowned and admonished: "Ooh la la. To be a professional in Europe, maybe 49, 49.5."

I sensed that Pedro wasn't just sharing information. He was

testing the waters with this new team member. Better to feign ignorance, I decided, which wasn't much of a stretch anyway.

"How do I do that?" I asked.

"I have some special B vitamins," Pedro ventured, but the team doctor wasn't recommending those special B vitamins as part of my medical program. Not yet anyway.

"Maybe later," Pedro confided, "I will give you some."

I suspected that "B vitamins" was Pedro's code for performance enhancing drugs, including EPO — short for Erythropoietin — a banned hormone that stimulates the production of red blood cells. More red blood cells means fatigued muscles get more oxygen, which is the fuel so critical to endurance athletes.

EPO is the human equivalent of high-octane fuel for Formula 1 cars. It allows an athlete to go longer and harder.

When the team deployed to Europe, I soon deduced that many of our competitors had team doctors like Pedro Celaya. These riders were super-charged, unflagging, and you could kill yourself trying to keep up.

My final race of the punishing spring racing campaign was the Tour of Romandie, a five-day stage race in Switzerland in early May. On one stage, cold rains descended on the main field of riders in the peloton. As the race progressed, the sky darkened and the wind and rain pummeled.

Some of the patrons — the seasoned veterans — of the peloton decided it was too cold to continue racing, so we all pulled over under a bridge while the patrons argued with the race promoter and race officials about whether to continue. Eventually it was negotiated that the race would resume, but the main climb would be eliminated because it was snowing too hard.

By this point I was completely frozen. You'd think growing up in Telluride, Colorado, would make me immune to the cold, but for some reason I did not handle it well. Nothing saps your energy like standing around, soaking wet, in thin cycling clothes. When we started again I could barely feel my hands and feet.

My teeth chattered together like those wind-up toys. I shook so badly my bike wobbled all over the road and I thought I was going to crash. I squeezed the brakes and pedaled in an effort to stay warm, but I just couldn't control my bike.

The mountains in Switzerland are massive, and the race organizers made sure we raced over some of them — weather be damned. Postal's designated race leader was Frenchman Jean Cyril Robin. He was a petite climber and I'm 6 foot 3, so my job was to keep him out of the wind and near the front of the race as we hit the mountains.

My size gave him a big draft so he was sheltered from the wind. The road leading to one big climb must have been one of the narrowest in all of Switzerland. It was hard to hold my position, and riders fought to stay near the front of the group.

Jean Cyril kept losing my wheel. Several times I drifted to the back of the peloton to find him and bring him back toward the front. After my third trip back, I screamed at him: "I'm killing myself to keep you at the front! Don't lose my wheel again!"

We crossed a narrow bridge and the road steepened. I needed to make sure no gaps opened up and he was near the leaders. I kept it in the big ring, pushing a massive gear to maintain speed and momentum. I went as hard as I could. Finally, after a kilometer or so, I delivered him to the front of the group.

Anaerobic from yo-yoing back and forth to get Jean Cyril, I promptly blew — I was physically spent. Nearly the entire peloton raced passed me and soon I was on my own. I climbed at a slow but steady pace, but before long the "broom wagon" was behind me. The broom wagon is literally a van with brooms attached to it. It is used to sweep up the stragglers at the very back of the race.

I finally recovered enough to catch the gruppetto — sometimes called "the laughing group" for the camaraderie common among these support riders. There is safety in numbers, and our group was roughly sixty riders strong. Someone had calculated exactly how fast we needed to ride to make the time cut. The plan was to climb at a steady pace and then go kamikaze on the descents and race the valleys between passes flat-out.

Hurtling down at breakneck speed was harrowing. This stage had a summit finish, and on the final climb we were behind pace. It looked like we might all be eliminated. The group began climbing in earnest. I stayed with the group, but a few other stragglers fell off pace. I made the time cut by mere seconds, but those behind were eliminated.

After the final time trial in Geneva I was exhausted and demoralized. I had spent most of my spring racing campaign lagging with the laughing gruppetto or, worse, in the gutter, forced out of the protective echelon of riders and fighting the wind at the edge of the road.

Pedro called me into his hotel room to discuss the next part of our season. He pinched my side. My skin stretched tight as a drumhead across my ribs.

"You need to gain a kilo or two!" Pedro scolded.

(When I later told my Postal teammate George Hincapie this he laughed and said, "You are the only person he has ever told to gain weight!" Spartan dieting was Pedro's usual prescription.)

"Take a week off the bike to recover but then start training hard for the second part of the season," Pedro said.

He handed me a calendar with a training schedule. There was a two-week block of training with 150 to 220 kilometers each day. On many days there were intervals and speed work at the end of the rides. It was a grueling regimen.

It wasn't the type of training you did clean. There were no recovery days, and he'd drawn stars and dots on each day — that was new.

Pedro handed me a Ziploc baggie filled with pills and glass vials of liquid. He picked up the calendar and explained the dots and stars; each dot on the calendar represented a pill, and each star represented an injection. I asked him what was in the baggie.

"Steroids," he said.

Now I was really nervous, so I tried to break the tension with a joke. "Are these going to make my balls shrink?"

Pedro chortled. "No, no, no. These are mild steroids, but you will go strong like bull — stronger than ever before!"

Strength was what I needed then, but not just for my body. That baggie was a fulcrum point for me. With each illicit injection and popped pill I could tip to the winning side, with the other cyclists who surged past their physiological limits.

And who cheated to get there.

Or I could reject Pedro's illegal medical program, likely get dropped from the team, and tip back, back to a rider who was competitive in clean American races, but who would never test himself against the best in the world: a failure in my eyes and others'.

It would be setting limits on myself as a competitor, whereas previously my upward trajectory had seemed limitless.

That baggie looked pretty innocuous, really.

When you want something badly enough you can rationalize choices, even really bad choices: a shady means to a glorious end.

I needed to decide who I was, and who I was willing to be, or not be.

Win True

CONTENTS

1   Define Yourself   1

2   Earn Your Breaks   13

3   See Where the Road Takes You   25

4   Claim Your Freedom   33

5   Approval Isn't Required   47

6   Knock on Opportunity's Door   55

7   Speak Your Mind   65

8   Lose and Learn   75

9   Win as a Team   99

10 If You're a Cheater You're a Liar   115

11 Make a Bold Move   131

12 Fall Down, Get Up, Repeat   135

13 Keep Your Options Open   141

14 Get Your Hands Dirty   149

15 Don't Be Silenced   159

16 Don't Assume Anything   165

17	It's Not Always Supposed To Be Fun	175
18	Own the Consequences	183
19	Sport as Proxy for Life	191
	Acknowledgments	199
	About the Authors	201

Chapter 1
DEFINE YOURSELF

*Circumstances may shape you,
but you make the choices that define you.*

We piled into our faded blue van — all three kids, my mom, and Telluride dad — to pick wild asparagus and attend church in Nucla, a speck of a former uranium mining town an hour away from our Telluride home. More importantly, Nucla was lower in elevation. After long, cold winters, we'd chase warmer spring weather down the mountain flanks.

I don't remember the specific sermon, but I remember I was itching to get outside. When the service finally ended, I sprinted to our van and grabbed my skateboard. The church was perched at the top of a long hill, and I started carving turns down the road. Out of the corner of my eye I noticed a girl running down the sidewalk. I thought to myself, *No way is a girl going to beat me down this hill!*

I straightened out the board and accelerated.

Twelve-year-old boys are not known for great judgment, and I was certainly no exception. The hill was longer — and steeper — than I thought. I soon was going so fast I started to get scared. My board got the speed wobbles and I made my second poor decision of the morning: I jumped off. I must have been going 20 to 25 miles an hour. I rolled and tumbled, limbs flailing, finally coming to a stop when my knee took the full braking force, slamming hard into the pavement. Grabbing my leg, I saw my kneecap was halfway up my thigh, and there was a big hole where it should have been. My dad ran down the hill, scooped me up, and carried me to the van.

I was in the hospital for seventeen days. My post-surgical recovery consisted of stretching, strength training, and cycling. The doctor said that since cycling was a non-impact activity, it would help me build strength and flexibility but would not be too strenuous for my knee. As motivation, Dad said he would pay me $200 if I would pedal the twenty-two miles from Telluride to Ophir and back every day that summer. He also bought me my first 10-speed bike: a black Peugeot similar to the bikes ridden by the pros in Europe.

My best friend, Tad Craig, joined me on most of those rides. Tad was my brother from another hippie mother. A year-and-a-half older, Tad had my same red hair and freckles, but blue eyes instead of my brown. (We looked enough alike that years later my nineteen-year-old-self used Tad's driver's license as a fake ID and it passed muster with a cop in a Telluride bar.)

Tad and I were rambunctious partners-in-crime. We built LEGOS, played cops and robbers, and ski raced together. But with my wrecked knee I had some work to do to get back to shenanigans-shape. Tad was game to be my rehab riding partner.

At first, my range of motion was so limited I could barely push the pedals, and climbing the hills around Telluride was slow and painful. The climbs seemed huge and the eleven miles to Ophir may as well have been as far as the moon. Slowly, however, I began to build strength, and my endurance increased. Tad and I usually made these rides into all-day affairs. Just outside of Ophir was a spring that someone had tapped with a pipe, which made it easy to fill our water bottles. There were very few cars on the road, and we never felt in danger.

That summer I fell in love with cycling. The 10-speed bicycle strengthened my body and galvanized my confidence. I discovered on the centrifugal force of two wheels a natural physical rhythm that had eluded my lanky body and big feet, which didn't so effectively navigate basketball courts and football fields.

But it wasn't just the physicality of cycling that felt right for me, it was the open road that helped me air out and organize my thoughts. My time spent riding planted the seed that if I could accomplish a goal of pedaling my bike twenty-two miles a day, I could set bigger goals someday. And I did. Eventually I would ride far enough and fast enough to compete around the world first as an Olympic athlete and then as a professional cyclist.

None of my future success as an athlete would have been possible without that first bike. The bike helped me recover from a horrific injury that still affects me to this day. My Telluride dad, Bill Kees, and I were talking about that seminal summer of riding the other day.

"You rode your bike every day — didn't miss a day," Bill said. "That was really impressive for a young man to be that focused and that determined."

"I can see why you were surprised I stuck with it," I replied. "I mean I could be a … challenge … sometimes."

"I knew you were focused, but I didn't really realize how determined you were and also how goal-oriented you were," Bill said. "You earned every penny of that $200, I'll tell you that. It was a little bit of a window into a much larger picture of you."

It really was a tale of two worlds — and two dads — in my childhood. My little sister, Lorraine, and I moved with our mom and step-dad — our Telluride dad — from Southern California to Telluride in 1972 when I was four. My Telluride dad had heard a new ski resort was opening in Telluride and was sure opportunity would follow — it just didn't follow very fast.

My mom, Susan Kees, and my biological dad, Roger Mercier — my LA dad — had just divorced, but I don't really remember much about that. We were poor in Telluride. My parents do well now, but we struggled then, and my LA dad was a corporate attorney and was well off, so it was a dichotomy between the two families.

When we first arrived in Telluride we didn't have a place to live, so we camped out for three months in the summer at 8,750 feet in elevation. Finally, my parents found a home for us. It was a 100-year-old dilapidated house in the isolated mining town where Butch Cassidy robbed his first bank. The house was in such disrepair that my Grandpa Emmett burst into tears when he saw where his daughter was living.

Telluride then was nothing like the high-end resort community it would become, attracting part-time celebrity residents such as Tom Cruise, Neil Young, and Oprah Winfrey. Back then it attracted ski bums and hippies. The Idarado mine was still open, so it was a culture clash between the blue-collar miners and the freewheeling hippies. My Telluride dad had spent the previous winter working in Aspen, so he knew how to survive in a ski town. The new Telluride Ski Resort opened in 1972, and Dad found odd jobs as a bartender, carpenter, and laborer.

Eventually he worked his way up to successful contractor and real estate agent.

I call both my dads "Dad." I think I was able to pick up distinct skills from each of them and distinct faults from each of them, too. Even though they're very different, they both made me the man I am today. I didn't make it easy for either one; I was a handful.

The two constants were my little sister Lorraine and my mom. Lorraine and I have always been best friends. She's two years younger, but she skipped first grade so we were just a year apart in school.

Mom was always there for me. We even share a birthday. Mom was an English teacher and counselor and is very much a free spirit. She transformed from a California beach girl to a Colorado mountain woman, brewing dandelion wine with one buttery bloom tucked behind an ear.

Mom's parenting style included a liberal dose of latitude for good behavior. If I wanted to go ski on a powder day during the school week, Mom had the philosophy that if you kept your grades up, you could take a day off here and there. In winter, we'd listen to public radio station KOTO in Telluride to hear if school had been canceled for a snow day, which is also a powder day to skiers. After one great snowstorm, there was no powder day announcement by KOTO and I decided to take matters into my own hands. Assuming my best adult voice, I called the radio station and said I was Principal Cleve Pemberthy and that school was closed for the day. The radio station called it, and the whole school got a free powder day. I still don't know if Principal Pemberthy knows I was that mystery impersonator.

Telluride was a great place to grow up because kids had so much freedom. We roamed like feral cats. Lorraine and I and a pack of friends would leave the house in the morning and our parents wouldn't have any idea where we were until we came home for dinner. There wasn't much to worry about in terms of stranger danger. Only about 600 people lived there then, and everyone knew each other.

We ran around in the woods, rode bikes, and rolled rocks down the canyons. Some of the things we did were dangerous; I can't believe one of us didn't get killed. I specifically remember an old suspension bridge that used to carry the town's water. The bridge spanned a canyon and it was probably 200 feet down to the bottom. The bridge was essentially a two-foot diameter water pipe with some wooden planks along the top. Most of the wood was broken apart — rotted — so just the pipe remained in places.

On a taunting dare — nothing's worse than being a chicken — we climbed across that decrepit bridge on our hands and knees. I was terrified — all but paralyzed with fear. The consequence of a fall was death, no question. I still start sweating in fear just thinking about it.

When I was five years old my Telluride dad taught me how to start a fire for a very practical reason: We had a potbelly stove for heat and I needed to know how to start it to keep the house warm. Not long after, Lorraine, who was three, and friend Timmy, who was four, and I set out exploring for the day.

We came across an old mine shack and found some Strike Anywhere wooden matches outside of it. Being the big kid —

showing off a little — I started lighting matches the way I'd been shown. I tossed the burning matches into the dry grass and the next thing I knew the whole wall of the structure was engulfed in flames.

Success! Wanting to finish the job, I went inside the building to light more matches and make sure the whole thing burned.

I didn't even realize what I was doing was wrong at first. I had only learned how to light a fire the week before. I thought it was the coolest thing in the world and didn't understand the consequences of it. Inside the building it was so hot the windows burst out of their frames, shooting glass shrapnel. I'm lucky I didn't get killed.

Back outside, we three preschoolers stood and watched the building burn to the ground. The flames must have been 40 or 50 feet high. Something in my larval brain triggered the realization that maybe I could get in trouble, so I started leading the other two kids nonchalantly down the trail to my house.

Dad was sprinting up the trail to the fire and passed me moseying the other way. He later told me that something clicked in his brain: *Why is this kid walking away from the fire?*

He turned to me and said: "Scotty, do you know anything about this? Did you have anything to do with this?"

I asked him, "You remember how you said if we tell the truth we won't get in trouble?"

He eyed me and nodded.

I said, "Yeah, I did it."

The police responded and there was this one guy, Marshal Everett M. Morrow, who was probably 5-foot-6 from his boot heels to the crown of his cowboy hat. Marshal Morrow was old-school law enforcement, and he told me if he ever saw me do anything like that again, I would be going to jail and my parents would be going to jail: I would never see my parents again. For the next few years I was terrified of him and would hide under cars if I saw him driving through town.

Years later my mom purchased a framed photo of Marshal Morrow at a garage sale. It hangs in my office today. I don't know if my parents were in on his scare tactics, but I imagine they were. I found out when I was older that someone had been living in that mine shack at the time, but he fortunately wasn't home when I lit up his house. The ruins aren't there anymore; the building burned to the foundation. This was July third, I know, because I clearly remember what happened the next day.

I was caught trying to light a pile of logs on fire while playing at a friend's house. A friend of my mom's caught me and told my parents. I couldn't talk my way out of trouble this time. I got one of the worse spankings of my life. To this day I remember that spanking. It wasn't abuse, but it was physically and emotionally painful. I can imagine how scared my parents must have been, thinking they had some little pyromaniac on their hands. At the tender age of five, and with my semi-frequent bed-wetting, I was two-thirds of the way to the FBI profile of a budding serial killer. Had I started torturing small animals, they really would have had cause for worry.

As it was, it was the Fourth of July and I was grounded from watching the fireworks. That was punishment enough. I haven't had any issues with fire since.

There were 265 kids in kindergarten through twelfth grade in the Telluride School District. My class, the class of 1986, had thirteen kids, and six of us went through school from kindergarten on up through high school together. I had a speech impediment — I stuttered — and in fourth grade I had to go to the special-ed room.

Gordy Gibson was the special-ed teacher. I was so humiliated that it only took me a few weeks to get out of that room — I knew I didn't want to stay in there. I don't even remember what the therapy was. Few people can believe I had a speech impediment because I speak pretty well today.

I was more in my element out-of-doors. In seventh grade my mom, then a teacher, took our class on a field trip, and we rode our bikes up to the Idarado mine and back. It wasn't a long ride; probably four miles, round-trip, from the school. I was the first one up the hill, to the mine, and on the way back we rode through the middle of town. Of course it turned into a race. I was going as fast as I could, in the lead, when a police officer cruised up behind me and sounded his siren.

"You're speeding and you need to slow down!" the officer blared over his loudspeaker.

I was pretty proud of that. My mom didn't think any further interaction with law enforcement was funny, but you can imagine that as a kid getting pulled over by a cop for speeding through town on a bike was pretty cool. That gave me seventh-grade bragging rights for a while.

I was by no means the popular kid or the athlete; I was the jokester. I got attention by playing practical jokes or getting in trouble — not serious trouble with drugs or alcohol, but I was a smart ass. In Mr. Polly's sixth-grade homeroom one day I was really fidgety and kept popping up out of my desk. It was just hard to sit still. I was clearly getting on Mr. Polly's nerves and pushing the limits of his generous boundaries of classroom management.

"Just stay in your chair!" Mr. Polly finally barked.

So I grabbed my chair and held it to my butt as I walked around the class. I technically was staying in my chair. Mr. Polly was not amused. The rest of the class burst out laughing, but Mr. Polly turned beet red. I had earned detention and had to stay after school and write, "I will not disrespect" over and over on the chalkboard. *The Simpsons* was my favorite show later on. Bart Simpson and I had the whole repetitive-writing-on-the-chalkboard-punishment-thing in common.

We didn't have a television when I was little. We finally got a basic, black-and-white TV when I was in middle school. It had one channel. We later got cable, but my mom only let us watch half an hour a day. I always felt left out because other kids got to watch a lot of TV. I never had any idea what show they were talking about at school. In retrospect, though, she was doing me a favor. She made sure we experienced the world instead of a screen.

Mom had wanted to take each of her kids on an individual trip during our sixth-grade year — me, Lorraine, and little brother Blake — but after I blew out my knee Mom waited a year and took both

Lorraine and me to Mexico's Yucatán Peninsula when I was in seventh grade and Lorraine was in sixth.

For three weeks we freely roamed the tropical beaches, Mayan ruins, and cenotes — underground freshwater pools and limestone caves — of Tulum, Cozumel, Isla Mujeres, and Chichén Itzá. This was 1980, and the Mayan archeological treasures there were not protected as they are now. Lorraine and I climbed the stone steps of the 98-foot-tall, 1,500-year-old El Castillo pyramid, also known as the temple of Kukulcán. I am terrified of heights, and when I got to the top and looked down, I had that dizzying cat-in-the-tree panic: How the hell am I going to get back down?

Also at the temple, a full-sized jaguar, carved from jade, stood guard at an underground cavern. The jaguar had empty sockets where its ruby eyes had been, the precious gems plucked by thieves. We stayed out of school two weeks after our return, because we'd caught hepatitis from the water and were contagious.

By that time my Telluride dad was doing well in real estate, so he and my mom agreed she could save her teaching salary and do whatever she wanted with it. She became a counselor later on, after getting her master's degree from Western State College. I can't imagine how hard that was raising three kids and making the five-hour roundtrip drive from Telluride to Gunnison week after week.

Telluride was a safe and familiar cocoon, but Mom made sure all three of us kids spread our wings. She always believed that travel experience is as educational as academic acumen.

"We live in such a small little valley here that it is almost a sanctuary," Mom explained to us. "I want you to experience life outside of this box canyon."

Mom continued stashing her money and one day announced: "Okay, I saved up. We are going to live in Europe for six months."

My dad would have preferred investing the money in real estate or buying a new car, but Mom stood firm, "Well, you don't have to go, but the kids and I are going to live in France."

Mom took a French immersion language course and off we all went, including my initially reluctant Telluride dad, to live for half a year in France. Our temporary home was Argentière, just outside of Chamonix. The school Lorraine and I enrolled in was a ski academy, which meant we got out of our lessons each day at 1 p.m. to ski. We got season passes for $50 and could ski dozens of resorts and several hundred lifts. We all tried to learn the language, to mixed results. Sometimes it was only our family who could comprehend each other's attempts at broken French.

As typical Telluride hippies, we camped a lot, and our trip to France was no exception. During spring break on a road trip we camped under a bridge in the south of France.

My mom gifted me a lifetime desire to travel and explore, and a fluidity to adapt to different cultures.

Thanks to my family's encouragement, skiing and cycling became second nature. But that athletic ability didn't necessarily translate to other sports. After we returned home, I didn't play basketball at Telluride High School, even though I was the tallest kid in school. I was 6-foot-1 then, but gangly and uncoordinated. I did play soccer, and our team went undefeated one season, but I mostly rode the bench. I probably weighed 140 pounds. And I had a wrecked leg from my skateboarding injury and couldn't run or jump very well.

There was not a person in town who would have thought I would be a great athlete, ever.

I was always reasonably smart, but ski racing, not schoolwork, was my love. Inspired by all my time on the slopes, I dreamed of being an Olympic ski racer, but the knee injury put an end to that. If I'm honest, though, I really didn't work hard enough. Lots of ski racers have overcome significant and frequent injuries. I loved skiing, but I was lazy and didn't do much offseason conditioning.

Skiing was a way of life in Telluride. By the time I was six years old I had skied all over the mountain with no parental guidance at all — getting on and off lifts by myself and slicing through heavy stands of conifers. Tad and I skied together all the time. I don't remember how I learned to ski, I just did. Skiing in Telluride was like breathing: Everyone did it and you took it for granted. Tad and I must have skied nearly a hundred days a year.

My favorite ski race event was the slalom. My mom wouldn't let me do downhill because she thought it was too dangerous, which irritated me. I got pretty good at the slalom but I was nowhere near world class. In cycling I would have been the equivalent of a Category 2 racer. When you are a Category 4 you think a Category 2 is pretty good, but when you are a pro a Category 2 sucks. There is a big gap between the two.

Back then, Telluride Ski Resort was a small mountain. It only had five lifts and struggled to survive. Mostly locals skied Telluride until it was discovered by tourists and celebrities in the 1980s. Once neighboring Montrose built a local airport that could accommodate jets, Telluride was on the international radar.

It didn't matter to me that the scenery was astounding or that people came from all over the world to ski Telluride, when I graduated high school I just wanted to get the hell out of there. I wanted to get far from home and experience a completely different community. I applied to and chose Berkeley on a whim. I was applying to UCLA, where both my parents had graduated, but the University of California system let applicants apply for two schools on the same application. I wanted a new adventure and Berkeley, outside of urbane San Francisco, seemed like a good option.

I also was able to continue my ski racing "career" at Berkeley, but it was a club team, mostly a beer-drinking team. Attending Berkeley was pure default and dumb luck. When I realize now how hard it is to be accepted, it's amazing to me that I made the cut. I had some things going for me: I was valedictorian of my class of thirteen; my family had lived in Europe for six months; and I had good grades and test scores.

I had always been Mr. A-, doing just enough to do pretty well, but not great.

I guess A- was good enough for Berkeley.

Win True

Chapter 2

EARN YOUR BREAKS

There are no free laps in life.
The only way to get a break is to earn it.

My LA Dad came to Telluride to attend my high school graduation
and we left on a three-week cross-country bike trip the next day. I
was totally hungover, thanks to an ice-cold keg of Coors Light the
night before. Back then you could drink 3.2 beer at eighteen in
Colorado. Our principal and high school history teacher tapped the
keg at our graduation party at classmate Jonny Fisher's house. On
top of the pain of my throbbing hangover, I'd had my wisdom teeth
pulled four days earlier.

Neither my LA dad nor I had trained much for this preplanned
bike trip. Actually, I hadn't trained at all. The day we left was literally
Day One of my training. But I was an active teenager; the adjustment
was easier for me. My dad was forty-eight, with a desk job, and he
lived at sea level. Regardless, we got on our bikes — me with a
swollen jaw and throbbing head and Dad with a good chance of
getting altitude sickness — and pedaled out of Telluride.

My mom had primary custody of me following their divorce, so
since I was three years old my time with Dad had consisted of
visiting him every other Christmas and for four to six weeks in the
summer. Even then I shared his attention with my sister, Lorraine,

my stepbrother, Jon, my stepsister, Jill, and Michael, my half-brother. This would be different. This was just him and me, riding mostly side-by-side for twenty days.

The first day we stopped in Montrose — sixty-eight mostly downhill miles away — so that was an easy stretch. The next day we rode to Gunnison, another relatively easy day at sixty-five miles. But the third day was long. We rode over Monarch Pass, which tops the Continental Divide at 11,312 feet in elevation. Dad didn't tell me this then, but he was getting fluid in his lungs from altitude sickness, and he wasn't breathing well. He had a hard time sleeping those first couple of nights and his coughs sounded like a barking dog. He thought he might have been having a heart attack riding over the pass, he admitted later.

We stopped in the small mountain town of Salida — it must have been 5 o'clock — we pulled into a Pizza Hut and I thought we were done for the day. I was famished, so I stuffed myself with an entire pepperoni pizza. After dinner I expected we would find a motel and call it a day — we'd already ridden 110 miles and crossed the highest point on our route.

Dad said: "No. We're behind schedule," so we rode another fifty miles to Cañon City.

We did around 160 miles that day and it was 9:30 when we found a motel. We were winging it, but Dad knew we needed to average 110 miles a day to make it across the country and catch our flight home from Washington, D.C.

Thinking back on it, I'm about the same age now my dad was then. He had a demanding job as general counsel for Denny's restaurants and five kids to raise. I'm not sure how he was able to get away for so long, but I remember he made phone calls where he could along the way to keep in touch with the office. And this was before cellphones, so he was calling from motel rooms or pumping quarters into gas station phonebooths.

Later, my dad said people would say to him, "I can't believe at forty-eight you went and did that for three weeks!"

He would respond, "I can't believe an eighteen-year-old did that, really."

We took Highway 50 most of the way east. If the U.S. were a hoagie bun, Highway 50 is where you'd slice it, pretty much dead center, through the breadbasket of eastern Colorado and Kansas, then straight across Missouri, Illinois, Indiana, Ohio, West Virginia, and Virginia. It was just us, out in the open, exploring new territory and making up our own fun.

One day in western Kansas we watched a massive summer thunderstorm closing in on our right, which would have been to the south. It started pounding down rain. This was a rainstorm of biblical proportions — sheets of water drenched us and the wind was ferocious. With no shelter to be found, we put our heads down and pedaled on. I was a bit behind my dad at this point. A huge tractor pulled up, with wheels that had to be 10 feet high. As it was passing, I got behind it and drafted a giant rubber wheel.

The tractor and I caught up to my chugging-along dad and passed him.

I yelled out, "Hey there!" with a goofy grin on my face.

So Dad watched his kid ride by, drafting behind a humongous tractor. The wheel was probably 3-feet wide, so I had a perfect draft. The other wheel was in the mud on the shoulder, and the body of the tractor itself had to have been about eight feet off the road. That meant Dad had no draft, and he was getting splashed with mud. I could tell he was getting pissed, but I wasn't giving him my wheel. We found out later that storm was the start of a tornado — the tractor may have saved our lives.

You start inventing your own entertainment when you're on a bike all day, alone with your thoughts. One day I envisioned Dad was the peloton of the Tour de France, and I had to attack. In my imagination I was in the breakaway, leading with the patrons. He would get irate because I'd go miles up the road. Once he'd finally catch up with me he'd be pissed off.

I just explained: "Dad, I'm doing intervals. I gotta train!"

Another day, with my mind wandering, I wrote a commercial jingle. It was about cats and it went like this: *I wish I were a kitty cat —*

cats have so much fun — because they eat, sleep, and play each and every day! Suffice it to say that Madison Avenue never came knocking on my door to buy that little ditty. It's still stuck in my head all these years later.

One day I couldn't believe my eighteen-year-old eyes when I spied a roadside fireworks stand selling firecrackers and bottle rockets — the kind of pyrotechnics that were illegal in Colorado. We still had well over a thousand miles to go, but I bought 15 pounds of fireworks — bricks of Black Cat firecrackers and bundles of cellophane-wrapped bottle rockets. I tossed out clothing to make room.

This was 1986 and you could fly on an airplane with fireworks. I pedaled that illicit treasure all the way across the country and flew home with it in my bike bag. We were home by the Fourth of July, and I put my roadside purchases to good use. Maybe I was still a bit of a pyromaniac?

I had never been in the Midwest before. What struck me, coming from Colorado, was that I always assumed Kansas was pancake-flat. But eastern Kansas was gorgeous, with big rolling hills, and lots of lakes and trees. I remember being a little pissed off because I thought that from Monarch Pass on it would basically be downhill all the way to the Mississippi River. No such luck!

We crossed the confluence of the immense Mississippi and Ohio rivers in Cairo, Illinois. The long, iron bridge was snot-slippery from humidity. Up to that point, I had thought the Colorado was a big river, but compared to these water super-highways, the Colorado was more like a creek. Those immense, Midwestern rivers were like nothing I'd seen before. Years later, while working on a master's degree from the Harvard Extension school, I studied Cairo in a real estate class. It's a city in what's known as "terminal decline" from the loss of ferry transportation dominance as railroads moved goods and industry up the line.

But don't get the misimpression our trip was all pastoral tractor-drafting and river-reverie. There was the occasional gritty road rage to deal with. Outside Joplin, Missouri, a redneck in a pickup truck flying a Confederate flag really laid on the horn. We were on a freeway, which we generally tried to avoid, but we had to ride the freeway to cross town. It was rush hour, no less.

This pickup truck blew past us, and I flipped off the driver as soon as he exited the offramp.

The truck skidded to a stop.

Shit.

(My dad remembers this incident with clarity, so let's let him tell it.) "You were a skinny kid, maybe 160 pounds, and I was a forty-something corporate guy," he reminded me.

(Here's where the story goes all Rambo.) "Lucky for us both, I was probably looking pretty grim," he said. "I had a lot of trail dirt on by that time. So I locked eyes and came up to the truck and the guy was about twenty years old and his frantic girlfriend was urging him, 'Come on, come on, let's just go!' They drove off, and we still had twenty-five miles of kind of foothilly, Ozark riding. I was thinking they were going to go get some baseball bats or something. It worked out, but when we stopped that night I said: 'You know, Scott, we've got one rule on this trip: Don't do anything to get my ass kicked.' "

I had seen my dad get in a fight years before, and I didn't want that for him either, even though I know he could have taken that redneck and a couple of his closest buddies. When I was about ten years old, my dad took Lorraine and me to the Hermosa Beach pier on the Fourth of July. We'd walked out to the end of the pier and were coming back when these punk kids started throwing fireworks up on the pier from the beach down below. From their reaction, they thought it was pretty funny to startle us.

My dad didn't think it was funny at all.

Dad yelled at them, "Don't throw those fireworks at my kids!"

One cocky teenager shot back: "Oh yeah? What are you going to do about it?"

And Dad said, "Well I'm going to come down there and kick your ass!"

So, of course, this punk kid tossed another one up on the pier at us and my dad went ballistic. My dad doesn't bluff; I think I inherited that from him. He jumped down and wrestled that kid to the ground. He had one of the kid's arms twisted behind his back and his face pushed in the sand. My dad was a fighter. He also was a bit of a hothead then.

People who don't have kids don't understand how fiercely protective parents can be. When something like that happens, a dad's not fighting for pride, it's his protective instinctive: *Don't fuck with my kids.* After flipping the bird that one time in Missouri, I didn't put my dad in the position of having to defend me for the rest of the trip. Lesson learned.

In Kentucky, at a convenience store to refill water bottles, we met up with a dad and his son, who looked my age, with reddish-blond hair. The dad told us the tap water wasn't safe to drink. Instead, he asked his son to fill a pitcher with clean well water and make lemonade. Two guys on bikes and wearing Spandex were an anomaly at that time. Regardless, the four of us sat down on the convenience store porch steps together. I talked to the kid, who also had just graduated high school, and my dad talked to the dad, who was a coal miner. The kid said he was going to be a coal miner, too. That's when I was struck by how fortunate I was.

We'd both grown up in mining towns, but this kid most likely was going to be a coal miner for the rest of his life, while I had other options. Mining pays well, but it's a hard way to make a living. This made an impression on me. For the first time, I was really grateful to be going to college. My family might have struggled when I was growing up, but that was just the start, not the end, for me. My world seemed wide open, compared to his.

Spending all that time together, on the bikes all day, eating all our meals across the table from each other, flopping in motel rooms at night, my dad and I did get closer — sometimes closer than I wanted to be. An unfortunate choice for my dad, he wore tightie-whities underneath his cycling gear — a rookie mistake. You're supposed to be in your birthday suit under your cycling clothes, to avoid chafing. This bunching cotton from his tightie-whities didn't just give him blisters, it gave quarter-sized holes in his flesh on either side of his butt cheeks where the saddle rubbed.

But he didn't quit. I mean I've had saddle sores that weren't nearly that bad and it's incredibly painful. We still had several days to go, and we were riding six to eight hours a day.

He rode the last 400-plus miles sitting on open wounds.

We ended our ride in Jamestown, Virginia, then flew out of D.C. to our respective homes in California and Colorado: he back to the corporate world, and me to prepare for college.

That trip more deeply ingrained how cycling played an integral role in the milestones of my life. And I itched for more adventures. Between my mom's value of international travel, my Telluride dad's encouragement of independence, and that cross-country trip with my LA dad, I developed the confidence to travel and just figure things out as I went.

Over those three weeks on the asphalt, I also finally bonded with my dad. I came to respect, trust, and understand him. I saw him as a man, and not just as my dad.

Dad grew up very poor, in the housing projects of Long Beach. His father was a longshoreman, born in Minnesota. Dad's mom died in childbirth, and he was first raised by an aunt, his mom's sister.

Years later, I asked my dad what had given him the idea of taking me on a cross-country bike ride in the first place. I don't remember this teenage exchange at all, but he recalls it in vivid detail.

We'd started riding bikes together when I was fourteen or fifteen when I'd visit him in California. He was really getting into cycling then. At that point I didn't really care for my dad very much because I was still angry with him over my parents' divorce. I felt like he'd abandoned us, even though we were the ones who had moved away. From my teenage, self-centered perspective, he was living this carefree high life in LA while we were struggling in Telluride.

The way I looked at it, my mom had put him through law school, and then he'd broken it off right when things were turning around for them. I mean, it's obviously not that black-and-white, but as a kid, that's the way I saw it.

So this was my dad's explanation as to why he'd suggested this grueling, inconvenient cross-country ride with me.

"It started out as kind of a terrible challenge," Dad said. "We had that place in Southern California, part of Lake Arrowhead, and you came in the summer to visit. We were riding our bikes up to another lake called Big Bear Lake, which was a mile up the road. I felt a lot of resentment from you — a right and wrongness — like maybe it was not right for your dad to leave your mother. There was a little bit of edginess throughout that parental relationship all along. So we were riding bikes up to Big Bear and casually talking about how you were going to graduate from high school the next year."

"You turned to me and said, 'Are you even going to come back to my graduation?' "

"I don't know how the topic worked its way around to that, but it was cast out as a challenge. I casted back and suggested we take a bike ride across the country after you graduated. It anchored the relationship, that trip. It was a commitment we made to each other and one that we saw through."

Back in Telluride, I filled my last weeks before college with races. Transportation was courtesy of the old family van, which I christened the "Banshee Mobile." It wasn't my first time turning the wheel of the Banshee Mobile down the highway. Throughout high school I'd traveled with racing friends in the van.

Jake Sucharski, Fletch Schuler, and I had entered a few races across Colorado in high school. Jake and Fletch were fourteen and fifteen when we started, so as the older sixteen-year-old, I was the only one who could legally drive. I had a tendency to fall asleep behind the wheel when I was tired. Jake and Fletch were terrified that I would kill us, so they'd poke me with a stick or slap me to keep me awake. One time I was so exhausted that Fletch had to drive, even though he didn't yet have a driver's license. The Banshee was a manual drive with three on the tree but Fletch sucked it up and drove that thing through the Rocky Mountains for an hour or so to let me sleep.

We'd get our asses kicked in those early races. At a junior race in

Copper Mountain when I was sixteen the race organizers talked about how you could get a free lap if you needed one. It was a criterium, which was a timed race on a short circuit. With my short attention span — like most teenagers — I didn't listen to the full instructions. I heard "free lap," but I didn't hear the explanation of what that meant. So the race started, and I hadn't been training hard, and I was tired, and then I remembered this free lap thing. So I just pulled over and took a free lap and lay on the grass in the park in the middle of the course.

The pack came around and I was still tired, so I took three or four more free laps, got back in with the field, and got tired again. I took two more free laps, then got back in with the field and finished with the group. As I was checking the results I was disappointed to learn that I had been disqualified for taking unauthorized free laps.

It turns out free laps are only to be used if you suffer from a crash or mechanical failure, like a flat tire, not just because you're tired. You know that stitch you get from wind sprints? That was what I had. But I enjoyed my time lying on the grass, looking at drifting patterns in the clouds, and watching the race whiz by. I was thinking: *Free lap. What a concept! What a great sport!*

Guess there's no such thing as a free lap.

After I returned from my cross-country trip with my dad, and with a little more seasoning to us, Jake, Fletch, and I decided to try racing again. We loaded up the Banshee and crisscrossed the Four Corners of the Southwest. We were still pretty young and green, but we picked up a little worldliness along the way.

For instance, we didn't have bulk foods at our small grocery store in Telluride. When we saw open bins of snacks at a Steamboat Springs City Market grocer, we were sure we'd hit the mother lode. We had very little money. *This is the best thing ever!* we thought, as we sampled handful after handful of yogurt-covered pretzels and chocolate-covered almonds, debating their merits and trying to decide which one to buy.

A fed-up manager finally admonished over the intercom, "No grazing in the bulk foods!"

Outside of Steamboat we were driving through icy, piercing rain when we spotted a guy in a dark-green poncho hunched over against the elements, hitchhiking alongside the highway. We stopped and picked him up — it was really miserable out and we felt bad for him — and got our first good look at the hitchhiker in the luminescence of the Banshee Mobile dome light. The hitchhiker's eyes and cheeks were hollow, sunken. He didn't look normal.

This is the stereotypical start to a horror movie, I concluded too late. The hitchhiker told us he'd been walking all day, that nobody would pick him up until we did, and — true to horror plot development —he'd just gotten out of prison the day before.

Either Fletch or Jake — I was too freaked out to sort out the details, being the responsible one behind the wheel — casually reached for a big stick lying on the floorboards of the van, in case he had to strike our haunting hitchhiker with it. But the sallow-eyed hitchhiker turned out to be very polite, and we eventually dropped him off, drama free, at his destination.

We thought twice about picking up hitchhikers after that, but usually did anyway.

We were obsessed with all the pros and with Italian gear, in particular. Colnago was the brand of bike we thought was the best. Of course, they were all steel bikes back then, not the hyper light carbon ones like today. We raced the Mount Evans Hill Climb, which is some twenty-eight miles up the highest paved road in North America. Mount Evans is a Fourteener outside of Idaho Springs, Colorado. The climb is brutal. I think I got sixth place there. That was probably my best finish of that summer, but I was riding Category 4, or Juniors, so it was not an impressive result.

We had the Banshee Mobile at the top, and we gave a pro named Bjorn a ride back down. It was a bone-chilling 28 degrees. Bjorn looked like frozen hell. He had iced snot all over his face. It didn't matter to us. We thought he was the coolest guy in the world, of course, because he was a pro. I think he had finished Top 15 or something like that. That was our experience with the pros— we got to give one snot-plastered pro a ride in the Banshee Mobile.

22

It's weird to reflect back now. Jake, Fletch, and I idolized these pros, like Ron Kiefel. We talked about them all the time. Then, five years later, I was one of those guys. I can't comprehend it, really. In a way I took it for granted because it just happened, but it's still amazing to me that it happened at all.

It shouldn't have happened. We were not that good. We were just kids, and we didn't train that hard. I had ridden across the country, so I had a huge amount of base miles, but I was slower than dirt. Make that mud. Or quicksand. You get the idea.

We only did three or four races, which we discovered by reading a calendar of races in the back of Velo News, published in Boulder. It's a website now, but back then it was newspaper-print black-and-white.

We were in the right place, though. Cycling in Colorado was taking off. The Coors Classic, based in Colorado, was the biggest race in America. Greg LeMond had won the Tour de France that year, so bike racing was brought to the forefront of American sporting consciousness for the first time. With the exception of LeMond, most of the biggest pros in American racing were living in Colorado. We had Davis Phinney, Ron Kiefel, Roy Knickman — all the 7-Eleven guys. They were the first American-registered team to compete in the Tour de France.

Bryan Miller helped us out a little bit then, and later on he took an interest in my racing career and was a huge help to me. Miller was the only professional cyclist in Telluride at that time and was a big inspiration. He was one of the top climbers in the American peloton. As an occasional training partner, he helped me understand what it took to be a top-notch climber. One thing he said still sticks with me to this day. He said: "When you're really suffering, that's the best time to attack. Because if you're suffering, everyone else is too."

Jake, Fletch, and I never had any money for motels, but we'd crash on friends' floors or camp in the van for the six- to eight-week season. It was totally unsupervised. Here I was, an eighteen-year-old kid in charge of a fifteen- and sixteen-year-old. Our training largely consisted of trying to wipe each other out. Of the three of us, I had the most experience racing, having raced a couple summers by then. As the expert, I was demonstrating to these youngsters one day how to corner — just flying around a corner in Mount Crested Butte — and I wiped out so badly I needed ten stitches in my right elbow.

The following morning I raced with bandages on my arms and legs; I was pretty banged up. In cycling, unless you have a severely broken bone, you keep racing.

I really didn't think too long-term about my cycling goals, other than I was always hoping to earn enough points for an upgrade. You got points if you were in the Top 6, and you had to get like fifteen or twenty points to upgrade to the next level. My senior year in college I placed sixth in a race in Marin County. I was so stoked! I felt like I had just won the Tour de France. I was ecstatic that I had earned a single upgrade point because I knew that summer I was going to race and I wanted to get to a Category 3, which in golf would be the equivalent to a guy who shoots an 80 — a good amateur but really not that good in the grand scheme of things.

This chapter is dedicated to the memory of Jake Sucharski.

Chapter 3
SEE WHERE THE ROAD TAKES YOU

*Don't expect to know what the destination looks like
when you're just starting out.*

After my college graduation in 1990, my Telluride dad suggested I come home for the summer, bang nails to earn some cash, and race bikes along with my fifteen-year-old brother, Blake. Dad sponsored us by giving us entry fees, gas money, and use of the Banshee Mobile to drive to races. Blake and I had to earn prize money to pay any remaining expenses.

First, Dad took me on a three-week college graduation trip: camping riverside and rafting whitewater in the Grand Canyon. Seeing the splendor of the canyon from a raft for three weeks is something I'll never forget. We flipped the raft in Lava Falls. It was my dad's first time flipping a raft after years on rivers. We'd scouted the rapid for hours, but we missed our line and went right over the falls.

The canyon is about as far removed from modern civilization as you can get. Sharing a raft with my dad for three weeks was a great father-son bonding experience. After the trip I started my day job as a construction laborer and my side-hustle as a semi-professional cyclist.

I didn't expect much would happen with racing except that Blake and I would have a summer of adventure in the van. Sitting on a raft for twenty-four days wasn't exactly ideal race training. Rafting is called "float and bloat" for a reason.

I'd entered a few races my freshman year in college, but I really got into cycling my senior year, on the Cal C Team. I earned enough points to move up to the B Team, but that was it. I got a couple of podium placings, but I wasn't training hard and wasn't showing much promise as an athlete. I was your typical, distracted, frat boy college student: drinking beer because it was fun and studying because I had to. While at Berkeley I was a spectator at the Coors Classic, where the prologue went up to Coit Tower in San Francisco. Ron Kiefel won the prologue. Seven years later we were professional teammates and Ron was giving me descending lessons. But I would never have guessed that then.

My plan after college was to race for the summer and save up construction-labor money for a long backpacking trip around the world, starting in the fall.

Blake and I carried boards in the morning and rode bikes in the afternoon. I had no idea what I was doing preparing for racing; I just figured I would train in the mountains. Nearly every day we did intervals up the hill to the airport of around two to three minutes. I had no training plan and would just ride until I puked. Then I would do a few more hill repeats for good measure. At the time I thought I was being a bad ass, but years later I learned that vomiting during a workout is typically a sign of lack of fitness. We were privateers: cyclists who raced on their own without the financial and coaching support of an organized team.

My dad explained why he thought Blake and I were a worthy racing investment.

"We've always had some kind of van," he reminded me. "Back then we had an old Dodge 6-cylinder. As a family we went to Yosemite and different places to go rock climbing and do river trips. We are an athletic family and an outdoors family. We'd pack everything in the van and sleep in it when you kids were young. And then when we needed more room we'd set up a tent next to the van."

"So after you graduated from college, I realized that this is the last summer you'd be spending with your little brother, so why not sponsor the two of you? You come up with a budget and I'll sponsor you guys, but the only thing I'm going to require is that you take the van and you sleep in the van the way I have done it. I want you to get a sense of what that independence is like."

I made a race budget, and Blake and I spent summer weekends driving to Arizona, Utah, Wyoming, and the Front Range of Colorado for races. To my surprise, I started winning races right out of the chute. It became clear that I might have a future in cycling, despite my low expectations and lack of experience.

Blake and I had all kinds of adventures — not necessarily the enjoyable kind. One time the Banshee Mobile broke down on the freeway in Denver.

I called home. "Dad, can you come out and get us?"

He started laughing and said: "You guys can figure it out. That is exactly why you are in the van."

Blake and I also broke down in the desert outside of Flagstaff, Arizona. Something happened to the gas pedal. The motor was running, but when I'd try to give it some gas to accelerate, the van would just idle. We didn't want to spend the night stranded there, but neither Blake nor I was very mechanical. We realized the pin connecting the gas pedal to the lever that goes to the engine had broken. We found some baling wire and jerry-rigged it. It worked and we got back on the road.

I didn't expect the racing season to be as successful as it was. I hadn't shown promise and had never gotten results either as a junior or a collegiate cyclist. Of course, I'd never trained hard either and had only dabbled in the sport. But all of the sudden I won nearly every race I entered. Within six weeks I had progressed from a novice amateur to an elite amateur. The only thing I can attribute that to is, at twenty-two, I must have grown into my body and I also really put a lot of hard work into my training.

When I'd started out at eighteen I'd been very, very skinny, which should have been good for cycling, where riders keep themselves light, like horse jockeys, but I didn't have good bike-handling skills. I didn't know how to race my bike. More importantly, I didn't have a work ethic and I hadn't learned how to suffer. Suffering is what makes a great cyclist: the ability to absorb pain and to find the willpower to dig deep and attack your competitors.

Four years later I got a restart to cycling. I still didn't have very good bike-handling skills, but I put in the work and got strong. I learned to suffer and could get myself in position where I was always at the front of the race. I rocketed up from a Category 4 to a Category 3 to a Category 2 in five races over those six weeks. I got all my Cat. 4 to Cat. 3 upgrade points in just one stage race: the Moots Classic in Steamboat.

I flatted in the time trial but still managed to get second. I remember playing mind games with myself after the flat to push myself harder and harder. I won the road race, the criterium, and the overall. I had won enough points just in The Moots Classic to earn my first upgrade: from a Cat. 4 to a Cat. 3. I was still doing dumb things like attacking from the front, which is stupid because everybody can see you; there is no element of surprise and you don't have full speed when you hit the front. But I'd inevitably get a big gap between the peloton and me, and most of the time I could hold it to the finish line.

I rode very aggressively — very stupidly, quite frankly — but I had the legs and lungs to make it work. I also learned that if you are aggressive you put yourself in a position to win.

Years later, I won a Moots titanium road bike in a raffle following a Telluride-to-Moab fundraising ride. It was the most beautiful bike I've ever ridden. Moots is based in Steamboat Springs, and the handmade bikes are manufactured there. The welding was perfect — so perfect and smooth that you couldn't see seams on the frame.

My Cat. 2 upgrade came in Flagstaff, and that's where I met Bobby Stuckey, who is still a good friend to this day. Bobby was one of my big rivals in the Flagstaff race. He was from Flagstaff and had the hometown advantage. I had a great race and won three of the four stages and the overall. The first stage was a short prologue hill climb, which I smashed, with the fastest time of the day, including the pros. Bobby won the road race. He attacked with around ten miles to go and no one would help me chase him down. I blew the race to bits chasing him but was still unable to get him before the line, and two guys sprinted past me for the remaining places on the podium.

I was really just concerned about the time gaps as I wanted to maintain my lead on the general classification. The last stage was a criterium with a short but steep hill. I attacked on the last lap and won with a small gap on the peloton. Halfway through the race Bobby crashed and messed up his bike. Bobby was kind of agro back then. He was tall, muscular, and had a long, thick ponytail. He started yelling, to no one in particular, "I need a bike!"

My brother was standing nearby, and he offered Bobby his bike to use. So Bobby took Blake's bike, which was significantly too small for him, and crashed again. After the race, Blake explained to me how another rider borrowed his bike and wrecked it.

I found Bobby and said: "Hey, man. You gotta fix this."

The bike needed new handlebar tape. Bobby gave us $20 for the repairs and we became instant friends. After that, he'd come stay with me in Telluride and I'd go stay with him in Flagstaff. We ended up doing winter training camps at his parents' place in Scottsdale. Bobby is now a master sommelier with a James Beard Award. He co-owns Frasca in Boulder, which is ranked by Food and Wine as one of the Top 20 restaurants in the United States, so it's safe to say he got a little more refined.

The next race, in Boulder, gave me one of the worst weekends of the year. I got disqualified from one of the races for going over the yellow line. The race was a circuit race with a hard climb, but the roads were not closed to traffic, which meant riders could not cross the yellow line to advance, for their own safety.

I saw a group of riders who had been dropped after the first lap bridging back up to the peloton and I did not want the group to get bigger. I moved up to the front of the field to set a hard tempo, which I know now is really stupid. Not only would that have worn me out, but the riders who regrouped would have been dropped again on the next climb anyway.

The field was taking up the entire lane of the road, and I was not a good enough bike-handler to move up through gaps between riders in the peloton, so I crossed the yellow line and rode to the front of the race. A minute later the motorcycle referee came up to the front and kicked me out of the race. To finish off the bad weekend, not only did I not get good results, but our van also got towed. But setbacks aside, we were right in the thick of things.

Boulder was the epicenter of U.S. cycling then and it still is today. Training at altitude naturally raises your hematocrit, which improves your performance in endurance sports, including road racing, mountain biking, and running. The top marathoners live in or near Boulder. The best tri-athletes live there. There's a lot of synergy because these groups train together. Later, as a professional cyclist, I found that if I went home for two or three weeks to Telluride, which is another 3,300 feet higher than Boulder, I always competed much better, because of the training at an even higher altitude.

Near the end of August I entered my first race at the elite level with the pros. It was a stage race called The Tour of the Moon. The Tour of the Moon was one of the classic road races of the Coors Classic and was also the scene of one of the races in the movie *American Flyers*. Before the race, I ran into one of my best friends from high school, Lee. Lee is two years older, and we had skied and played soccer in Telluride. He definitely was one of the cool kids; I definitely was not. Lee is still one of my best friends. He approached me before the time trial and said: "Hey, Scott, what are you racing? The Cat. 4s?" Lee was a typical Cat. 3: arrogant, smug, and not as good as he thought he was. I looked at him and said: "No. I'm racing Cat. 2s. " I can still remember the look of disbelief on his face. One of his lifelong goals was to be a Cat. 2, and I'd done it in half a summer.

The opening stage of The Tour of the Moon was a time trial along River Road outside of Fruita, Colorado. Bryan Miller warned me that spokes were slow and suggested I race with a disc wheel. He said that if I covered the spokes I should be faster. I had no money for special aerodynamic equipment, so I got creative and cut some poster board paper and duct-taped it to the rim to make my own DIY disc.

The winner of the race had a time-trial bike, disc wheels, and an aerodynamic helmet. All I had was my homemade disc and clip-on time-trial bars. I placed third, just a handful of seconds from the win.

The final stage was a road race with two laps over Colorado National Monument, which is 20,000 acres of canyonlands between Fruita and Grand Junction. On the second lap I attacked the peloton on the climb to Cold Shivers Point — aptly named for the chills you get peering over the sheer canyon walls to the valley floor below. Four riders came with me and we worked smoothly together and quickly established a gap on the rest of the field. The overall winner would be crowned from this breakaway. Just as we passed Cold Shivers Point my saddle began to wobble and a few miles later it fell off. With the remaining climbs and descent, it was impossible to continue and I had to withdraw.

I needed the $100 saddle, so I turned around, picked it up, and put it in my pocket.

I was getting a lot of notice from Colorado people, especially when I was beating pros at time trials and up climbs.

But then I went and disappeared for seven months.

Win True

Chapter 4

CLAIM YOUR FREEDOM

*A walk around the world works wonders
for career planning.*

I pocketed enough money pounding nails over the summer to buy my freedom for a while. We all know the matriculation-into-adulthood-conveyor belt: Enter one side of the college stage, grasp diploma, shake hands, exit the other side of the stage and enter the workforce, preferably in a career related to the degree printed on your diploma, which for me was Economics.

It wasn't that I wasn't willing to work. I just wasn't willing to lock into a career yet. I knew that once I started working I'd be working for the next forty years, and I wanted to travel and have some spontaneous adventures before every day was a predictable 9 to 5.

My initial plan was to travel for two years. I'd start in Asia — spend six or seven months there — then head to New Zealand and get a job for a while. I didn't have enough money to cover two years of expenses, but I had college buddies who had worked on farms in New Zealand and Australia, and I knew I could find work there. From there, I'd continue west through Australia and Africa, finally going north to Europe.

However, after the successful summer of racing in the Banshee Mobile, I decided that maybe I didn't want to be away from cycling so long and lose all my momentum, so I changed my plans and decided to just travel around Asia. I sold my car, stashed the $2,000 I'd received for graduation, and threw in my savings. I think my total budget was $7,000 — in the form of a stack of American Express Travelers Cheques — to cover six or seven months. I didn't want to compromise for someone else's agenda, so I went on my own. I wanted to learn about myself and do my own deal. I bought a one-way ticket to Bangkok, with a stop in Japan, and planned to just wing it from there.

My college girlfriend, Jemetha Clarke, a Japanese major, was studying outside of Tokyo. I went to see her for ten days, toured around Japan on the bullet trains, and visited Buddhist temples. I really stood out in Japan. I towered over the Japanese, and with red hair, too. My college roommate, David Walker, was in Tokyo as well, teaching English. I knew if I needed to get a short-time job, I could make good money teaching English in Japan.

Bangkok was a nice hub for traveling through Southeast Asia and actually for traveling anywhere around the world. I passed through Bangkok three or four times as I crisscrossed Asia. Khao San Road is renowned among the backpacking community for inexpensive hostels and cheap beer. Of course, you hear about the widespread sex trade in Bangkok. I was not part of any donkey shows, but I would see these disgusting old dudes with very young Thai women. That part was really creepy, but the city itself was pretty spectacular, although every traveler should bring a little street smarts abroad.

A Thai woman once approached me on the street and asked for directions. I said: "I don't know. I'm not from Bangkok."

She feigned surprise, looking up at my red-hair-capped 6-foot-3 scaffolding. "You're not Thai?" she asked, skeptically.

I said, "Lady, I don't know what your scam is, but I'm obviously not Thai so you need to find somebody else." After Jamal Abdula I was wise to these types of scams.

My lesson in street smarts came courtesy of Jamal Abdula when I was a fresh-off-the-farm freshman at Berkeley. It was fall, and my dorm neighbor Hugo, from Orange County, and I were walking across campus to the library when we were approached by a nervous man with a heavy accent. He said he was South African. He walked and darted alongside us. Talking to him became more interesting than going to the library. However, if he saw a campus police officer, he'd get jittery and exclaim: "I've got to go over there! I cannot be seen walking with two white men!" My college admission essay was about apartheid, so I was sensitive to the struggle of South African black people. At this time, 1986, Nelson Mandela was still in prison, and dismantling the racist apartheid regime was a massive global movement. It had become part of American pop culture as well. Hugo and I, of course, wanted to help Jamal.

He confided his plight: His uncle had left him $50,000, and that's why he was able to travel to America. He held up a crumpled paper bag: "See? Here is $5,000 of it. The rest is in a suitcase at the bus station."

We couldn't believe it! It wasn't safe to carry money around like that, we scolded, it could get stolen. Put it in the bank, we admonished.

"No, no. I'm a black man! They keep your money!" Jamal refused, shaking his head.

The plot thickened. Jamal was going to meet up with a prostitute. We nodded. Well, he was worried about the prostitute stealing his $5,000. What should he do?

We tried to assure him: "Your money will be safe in a bank. You can get the money out whenever you want."

He did not believe us and asked us to prove it. We found a Wells Fargo ATM machine on campus and demonstrated with our ATM cards. "See?" Hugo withdrew $80. I withdrew $100 — about a third of what I had in my account. Jamal was undeterred. Ultimately, we agreed to watch the bag of cash while Jamal met up with a prostitute, then we would rendezvous at a park bench and return the bag to him.

Right before Jamal handed over the bag, he said: "Wait! How do I know you will fight for my money like you would fight for your own? You have a bag of my money, but your money is in your wallets. Put all your money in the bag with my money and we will pray together that nothing bad happens."

So we huddled up. It was right out of *Lion King*. Jamal chanted his prayer, and we closed our eyes and soaked it all in as if he were a Zulu chief. When properly blessed, we parted ways, and at the predetermined time Hugo and I went to the park bench and waited. And waited. And waited. We snooped through half a dozen of the seedier motels around campus looking for Jamal. No one had seen him. Back to the park bench. No Jamal. Finally, around midnight, we gave up and returned to the dorms, seriously concerned about Jamal's safety.

Curiosity got the best of us and we looked in the paper bag. It was filled with newspaper cut the same size as currency. Hugo was irate. I started laughing. When we reported it to the police, the officer nodded knowingly, "Oh yeah, that's the Jamaican Switch."

Jamal Abdula, or whatever his name really was, got our $180 and I got probably the most valuable lesson I learned at Berkeley. I'd never again be such an easy mark, and Jamal's lesson served me well years later on the streets of Bangkok.

From Bangkok, I planned to travel to India and then trek through Nepal. New Delhi was the first stop. I got off the plane and had no guidebook and no idea of what I was going to do. As I got through customs I was confronted with a mass of humanity, just thousands of people outside the airport. Bodies were packed as tightly as a tin of sardines.

I thought to myself: *I am twenty-two years old from Telluride, Colorado. What have I gotten myself into?* I didn't know where I was going to stay or what I was going to do. Fortunately there had been an Indian-American woman on the plane next to me, and I spotted her in customs. As we were gathering our bags she noticed that I was a little lost and she asked if I wanted to share a cab into the city. She suggested a modestly priced hotel where I stayed for a couple of days. After eating from a street vendor, I got the sickest I have been in my entire life. I spent three days huddled around the toilet puking my guts out. I must have lost ten pounds. I was thin to begin with; I was emaciated by the end of it.

Eventually, I was able to venture back out. Apparently, there was no trademark protection in India at that time. Instead of Coca-Cola, there was Caco-Cola in a red can with the exact same lettering. There was a fast food restaurant with arches like McDonald's, but it wasn't a real McDonald's. After being so sick, for the first week I would only eat Western food because I knew my stomach wouldn't be able to handle anything else. I found a hamburger restaurant with a huge photomural of mountains — it was the Sneffels range outside of Ridgway, near Telluride. A cross-country skier in the photo was a guy I knew from Telluride. It was the most bizarre thing in the world. Here I was in New Delhi, India, and it's not the Himalayas they're selling to tourists, it's Mount Sneffels, with a cross-country skiing Coloradan.

Poverty in New Delhi was evident everywhere — in the roaming mangy dogs, in the people sleeping in the streets. I know it's changed now, but back then it was unbelievably poor. People did what they could to survive. I spent a week there, walking around the city, checking out the markets and temples, and sidestepping people, dogs, and cattle. Brahma bulls were sacred, and bulls wandered the streets, starving to death.

I don't want to pass judgment, but the caste system seemed to be among the worst forms of discrimination. If you were born into a caste you were going to stay in that caste until the day you died with almost no opportunity to change your lot in life. I was chastised for giving a few dollars to a disfigured beggar because he was an "untouchable," or the lowest level of caste.

India was all about great poverty juxtaposed with great beauty. I did a day trip to the Taj Mahal, the white-marble "crown of the palaces" in Agra. The taxi driver I hired from the train station said he would drop me off and wait all day to bring me back. I tried to get the driver to leave, explaining I wasn't on any time schedule. He was insistent. He also had some scam going, which he relayed with great enthusiasm. After finding out I was from Colorado, he told me he had a cousin in Denver who was a jeweler, and he wanted to give me some rubies to deliver.

I said: "So let me get this straight. You want to give me these rubies, and when I get to Denver I'm supposed to look up your cousin who owns a jewelry shop and give him these jewels, and then he is going to pay me something for getting them there. How do you know I'm not just going to steal these?"

He looked astonished. "No, sir. I can see you're trustworthy. And if you steal them, I will call the police!"

I countered: "You really think the police in America are going to take a call from some guy in India and arrest me? I don't know what your scam is, but you need to find somebody else."

Jamal's $180 lesson was the gift that kept on giving.

I bought a train ticket east for the old fort city of Jodhpur, 155 miles from the Pakistani border, in order to see the sandy expanses of the Thar desert. I started to board what may as well have been a cattle car, jam-packed with people, chickens, and dogs. I had a second-class ticket with an assigned seat, but people were crammed everywhere — no one seemed to have assigned seats. The conductor stopped me and told me that particular car was third class, for Indians only. Outside their strict caste system, I and other foreigners traveled by comfortable sleeper car. You make friends along the way, abroad. There were fellow rail-riders from New Zealand, Canada, Australia, America, France, and England.

The James Bond movie *Octopussy* was filmed in Jodhpur, which is a popular tourist destination due to its historic forts, palaces, and temples. Jodhpur is called the "Blue City" because many homes in its oldest district are an intense light blue. Why people painted their homes blue is a matter of some debate. Indigo blue is associated with the Brahmins, India's priestly caste, some say. Others say the choice of blue is for practical, instead of aesthetic, reasons — the result of a lime wash with copper salt compounds applied to deter termites. Whatever the reason, the effect is phenomenal: an ocean of cool blue in the shimmering desert.

Seeking an authentic local experience, I went with four people on a camel safari. My camel was humongous. Once I climbed on, the guide took a wooden switch and swatted my mount. It took off sprinting and I basically had a "yard sale" — everything I had flew off in different directions. I hung on for dear life as my camel flat-out ran at close to 30 miles an hour. Items launched out of my backpack while I lurched back and forth. My pants got ripped to shreds. Everyone laughed, but I was terrified. You are way the hell up there on a camel —probably ten feet high — and they're fast and mean and don't listen. When going I couldn't get my camel to stop; when stopped, I couldn't get it to go again. It was worth the rough and cantankerous ride, though. The stars in the middle of the Thar desert were spectacular.

It was hot during the day and cold at night. In the evenings, guides built a fire and served spicy Indian food and hot tea. We slept on Indian carpets, and it felt like a scene right out of *Arabian Nights*. And during long, hot days, out of nowhere kids would show up with a cold Coke — or rather Caco-Cola — to sell. India gave me a sense of perspective and gratitude. In America, if you have drive, ambition, and a good work ethic, anything is possible. Obviously there are some limitations, but you can be resourceful. And while some have roadblocks, depending on their race or gender, there is plenty of opportunity in the U.S.

Then I spent six weeks in Nepal. While hiking the Annapurna trail, I met a guy named Brett, who lived in Berkeley and worked for North Face. We decided to stick together. The trek was an eighteen-day hike, starting at about 2,000 feet. It was really kind of a bizarre scene. We were literally in the tropics, among banana plantations, yet we could see in the distance the towering white-capped peaks of the Himalayas. Along the way, purple sticky marijuana buds grew like wildflowers. I wasn't much of a pot-smoker, but you could pick them and ask hosts at the guesthouses to bake them into a cake or brownies. We didn't summit any peaks, but the pass was over 18,000 feet high. We ascended slowly and took our time to acclimate. I can still remember the crisp blue sky, rocks piled into a massive cairn, and prayer flags fluttering at the summit of the pass.

On our descent we came across a woman from Singapore who

went up too quickly and was suffering from acute altitude sickness. Two people already were helping her, making a stretcher out of ski poles. One of them was a doctor from Germany, which was lucky for her. The doctor said we should get her down as quickly as possible because she was already starting to foam at the mouth. The four of us picked up the makeshift stretcher and ran down the pass as fast as we safely could. There was a small village several miles down the pass at an elevation of around 14,000 feet. We got the woman some hot tea and she began to feel better. She had a massive headache but was otherwise going to be fine. The German doctor said she was within half-an-hour to an hour of dying when we found her on the pass.

It's crazy the people you run across while traveling. Back in Bangkok, I ran into an old buddy of mine who had moved away from Telluride in middle school, Eric Davidson. His dad had been the publisher of the newspaper in Telluride, and when they sold the paper, Eric moved to Winter Park with his mom. I spotted Eric in a Bangkok bar — we both recognized each other immediately. He was teaching English in Japan and was in Bangkok between jobs. He's one of the smartest guys I know — very creative and intellectual. I'd planned on going to China a few days later as I started making my west back toward the U.S., but he asked if I wanted to go with him to Vietnam.

Why not? This was December of 1990. The American consulate in Bangkok suggested we not go to Vietnam because we didn't have diplomatic relations with them. We were still willing to risk it.

"Well, if you do go, and you get into trouble, go to the British Embassy," the clerk at the consulate advised.

We bought tickets and planned to go to Vietnam and Laos. We flew into Ho Chi Minh City, formerly Saigon, with the intent of staying for three or four days before heading north to Hanoi.

Christmas Eve in Ho Chi Minh was one of the more memorable nights of my life. Eric and I started our holiday celebration at a restaurant called Maxim's. It's still one of the best meals I've ever had. Vietnam used to be a French colony, and this was a French restaurant with Vietnamese influence. We had escargot, Caesar salad, veal, and wine. Our meal came to like $20. There was a small orchestra ensemble with a Vietnamese woman playing cello. We were instantly smitten with her. I remember her grace and beauty to this day, over thirty years later.

South Vietnam had a large Catholic population, and they celebrated Christmas Eve Mardi Gras-style, with a big parade and festival. Bags of confetti were a penny, and children ran around tossing it into the air and pelting people. We got into the spirit, throwing confetti at the kids, and they thought it was hilarious to have these big Americans running around playing with them. They loved us in South Vietnam — everywhere we went — because America was their former ally. It must have been about 10 when we encountered five white dudes with scowls on their faces lumbering along the sidewalk.

Nobody was throwing confetti at them. We suspected they were Russians, because Vietnam was a Soviet satellite state. We figured we may as well warm up the cold war, and what better way to get things started than with confetti? Eric and I ran up to them and pelted them with confetti — and questions.

"You guys are communists, aren't you? Russians!?"

They broke into grins. "Americanskis?" And we gave them the thumbs-up, like *let's party!*

Surprisingly, Eric started talking to them. Talking may be an overstatement, but he knew a few words of Russian. He also had a little Russian dictionary in his pocket that he thumbed through, to help us communicate. Turns out these Russians were merchant marines, with a curfew, and they wanted to sneak us onto their base to keep the party going. One of the guys told us to walk in the middle of their drunken scrum, like we were all hammered, and to not say a word. It didn't require too much acting; we were kind of drunk.

An old woman guarded the base gate, and she waved us through as if it were nothing out of the ordinary. It never occurred to her that two American kids were trying to sneak onto a Russian base. We spent the evening on a merchant marine ship drinking horrible rice vodka and listening to really loud rock — Quiet Riot and AC/DC — on a turntable. At about 4 in the morning, Eric concluded we needed to get ourselves out of there. He looked up "diabetes" in his Russian dictionary, and made up a story for the merchant marines that he had to leave so he could take his insulin. We took a cab to our hotel.

"So where to next?" I asked, primed for the next exploit.

"Cambodia," Eric said, seemingly picking a country at random. "How about Cambodia next?"

Neither of us knew much about Cambodia, so we went to the consulate to find out about a visa. The clerk didn't speak English, but Cambodia had been a French colony, and I spoke reasonable French from my time in Chamonix. Things were going well, and then they found someone at the consulate who could speak English. Now things were getting complicated.

He told me I had to write a letter explaining why we wanted to go to Cambodia, which was, by all accounts, a dangerous place. Pol Pot was still fighting a guerilla war in the jungles north of Phnom Penh. The Vietnamese had kicked the Cambodian communist revolutionary and leader of the Khmer Rouge out of Phnom Penh, but he was still fighting in the north. I came up with a story on the fly. I said we were graduate students at Berkeley and our master's program was on the political and economic systems of Southeast Asia. We'd studied capitalistic societies and socialistic societies, but our research would be incomplete if we didn't study Cambodia.

It was worth a try. We awaited the consulate's reply. Our original plan had been to take a flight to Hanoi — a thousand miles to the north — then to Laos, and then take the train back to Bangkok. Visas didn't seem likely, but we checked back the next day anyway and to our surprise found out they'd been approved. We couldn't believe our luck. We were so naïve.

We flew out of Ho Chi Minh City headed for Phnom Penh on the 28th of December, 1990. This would be no light-hearted adventure. Cambodia was a country still at war. We were the only tourists on the plane: two dumb kids. Everybody else was with the

Red Cross or were mercenaries —war junkies who were going there to fight — mostly French people, a few Brits, and a couple of Canadians. We landed at dusk, and the airport was dark. A man checked passports by the flickering flame of a cigarette lighter. We took a cab to a hotel and passed teenage boys on the streets, barefoot, shouldering AK-47s.

Shell-shocked French Colonial mansions braced the streets. Families squatted in the rubble with their donkeys and chickens. Phnom Penh was ravaged by war. Eric got sick, so he didn't venture out with me the next day. I paid $20 to a man who was probably in his fifties to give me a tour. He drove me to killing fields and mass gravesites thirty miles outside the city. I saw a pile of human skulls some 50 feet high. It was one of the most sobering things I had ever seen. It was heartbreaking. I watched a young girl fill a mortar shell from a broken fire hydrant spewing water into the streets. I met some of my guide's family. There were almost no men between the ages of eighteen and forty because Pol Pot had murdered so many.

But Eric and I were young and full of life, despite the specter of death around us. We went out on the town a couple of nights, but we were wary. We came up with a code word to alert the other to a sketchy situation. Denver Broncos running back Bobby Humphrey was our inspiration. If one said "Humphrey," we both knew to run like hell. We ended up at a club on the top floor of a building, and we were lucky to get out of the place. Scantily clad girls flocked to us, and the expectation was we would buy them drinks for their unsolicited attention.

And each drink cost $50.

Humphrey. Humphrey! HUMPHREY!

We realized we were not in a good place, so we didn't order anything. Knowing club bouncers weren't going to let us out without paying several hundred dollars, we watched and waited until we found an opening and then ran out of the club like our lives depended on it.

They probably did.

On New Year's Eve, Eric and I met up with some Canadian aid

workers and got kicked out of a Red Cross party for breaking glasses. I was into punk rock then and the Dead Kennedys' song "Holiday in Cambodia" was stuck in my head, and here we were in Cambodia. In celebration, we hurled glasses on the dance floor. I guess the Canadians weren't mosh pit fans. Well, not only that. I was purposely ticking off the Canadians because I previously had met a Canadian couple that was adamant about not being confused with being American, so I had taken an American flag and sewn it on my backpack so nobody would confuse me with being Canadian. I kept that American flag with me everywhere.

We had visas for five days in Cambodia, but once we left Vietnam our visas were canceled, so we had no way of getting back. We only had a one-way ticket to Phnom Penh and no idea how we were going to get back to Thailand. Eric's idea was that we could hire a guy to sneak us back into Vietnam by boat, down the Mekong River. That idea made me uncomfortable; I didn't want to sneak back into a country where we had no diplomatic relations. Eric was smart, but also a little crazy. We eventually were able to find a flight to Laos, which was just beginning to transform from a communist society to a more capitalistic one. It remained heavily influenced by the Soviet Union, but it was open to Americans.

I still have a pair of Russian binoculars and a Russian watch I bought at an open market in Laos. We crossed the Mekong River to the jungle of Thailand and took a train back to Bangkok. The whole trip was probably four weeks. Eric later went back to Myanmar, formerly known as Burma, with some mercenaries. He had a camera and wanted to get war footage. He was the only guy without a gun. For three weeks they traipsed through the jungle and made their way up the Mekong, trying to avoid getting malaria. They never found the Burmese. That is the kind of thing Eric would do. He later opened a bed and breakfast in Thailand. He is still there after getting his master's in criminology from the University of Colorado-Denver. He works on poaching and other crimes against animals.

Eric and I parted ways in Bangkok, and my girlfriend, Jemetha, joined me. We went diving off the island of Ko Samet, which is a national park just a few kilometers off the mainland of Thailand. The beaches there are like powdered sugar, the water is clear, and the coral reef is expansive. We had a relaxing, touristy beach vacation. The jungle grows right down to the beach, and the ocean is as warm as bathwater. It's no exaggeration to say it's a tropical paradise. You also can dive to shipwrecks sunk during World War II battles. We spent a couple of weeks traveling around Southern Thailand. Magic Mushroom omelettes were one of the island's culinary specialties, and we had a few of those, as well.

When Jemetha left, I was running out of money and ready to be home anyway. I headed east and finished my trip in China, Hong Kong, and Japan. The open-air markets in Guangzhou, China, were filled with exotic animals. I was into photography then and took a lot of photos. In the market, there was a raccoon in a cage I was trying to take a photo of, and the vendor poked it with a stick to try to get it to turn around and face the rear of the cage. Once the vendor had successfully maneuvered the animal, he grabbed it by the tail and yanked it out of the cage. He swung it up over his head and bashed the raccoon's head on the sidewalk to kill it. He screamed at me, "No photos!"

Later, I was staying in a Hong Kong hostel when a fire started at 2 in the morning. It was pounding down rain and all guests had to evacuate. With nowhere else to go, we slept on city park benches. After months on the road my zest for international adventure was dampening, too. I flew home from Japan in March of 1991.

All the while I had been traveling, in the back of my mind I'd been running through the options of what my next move in life should be. Should I commit to a career in the financial industry? That would make monetary sense. Should I pursue a graduate degree? That would make intellectual sense. They were both viable options that my family would approve of. After all, they'd sacrificed to get me this far.

But it wasn't just an either/or choice of launching a career or continuing my education. I kept coming back to a third, less lucrative and far less practical option, but one that spoke to my heart. With unrushed months to think about it, I had made up my mind to return to racing. I wanted to see how far I could go, how good I could be.

I didn't know it at the time, but I had some sort of a stomach bug gnawing at my athletic physique. I was thin. I was in awful shape.

And I thought I was ready to race.

Chapter 5
APPROVAL ISN'T REQUIRED

Even people who love you won't support every decision.

My skeletal frame touched down in the United States with $10 to my name. I started the '91 season training in Los Angeles, staying at my dad's place. I got the one job I could work around my training schedule: busing tables at a restaurant in Redondo Beach. I trained five to eight hours a day then bused tables at night. It wasn't ideal to be on my feet after riding all day, but I needed the money.

Dad gave me $600 to buy a beater car we named "The Yellow Bomber." The Yellow Bomber was the biggest piece of shit on the road. It was a 1972 Nissan two-door hatchback. The starter didn't work, so I had to park on a hill and roll down to jump-start it. It didn't have taillights, but the hazard lights didn't blink, so I'd leave them on and they functioned as taillights. The driver-side window wouldn't roll up or down. I don't think The Yellow Bomber would have been roadworthy in Tijuana, but it was all I could afford and it got me to my job and to the local SoCal races.

The Yellow Bomber was, not surprisingly, a magnet for cops, and I got pulled over on many occasions. One night, after a long shift, I got stopped just two minutes from my dad's house. The cops approached with weapons drawn. They let me off with a warning.

Luckily, top speed for the Yellow Bomber was just over jogging pace, so there was no chance of getting a speeding ticket. That incident with the police is a clear example of both profiling and white privilege. I was pulled over for no reason other than I was driving a shitty car and not harassed at all once they realized I was white.

There were good group rides leaving from Malibu, led by some of the local pros. One of the top domestic teams at that time was the Chevy LA-Sheriff's squad, and two of their pros were based in the South Bay of LA: Jamie Paolinetti and 1988 Olympian Dave Lettieri.

1991 was the last year Dave raced on the team, and he went on to be the Chevy LA-Sheriff Race Director. Dave recognized my commitment and made me feel welcome. He told me when SoCal races were happening and made sure I was included on what were pretty exclusive group training rides of 60 to 100 miles. He also gave me training and riding tips.

The rides started in Malibu, which was 25 miles from my dad's place in Palos Verdes. With my commute, I was getting in 110 to 160 miles each ride. Dave commented that with the extra miles from my commute, I was the only one in the group getting in enough miles to be competitive at CoreStates. I didn't know what he was talking about at the time, but CoreStates, in Philadelphia, was the professional road race national championship. His belief in me extended beyond these training rides. Just a year later, Dave would be the first to offer me a professional contract.

From Palos Verdes, I rode bike paths and beach streets north to meet the group. The amped-up LA scene was something new to me. Riding bike paths and dodging joggers, Rollerbladers, walkers, and tourists was a battle in itself. The paths were designed for leisurely rides on beach cruisers, not training rides at speed, so eventually I just avoided them and rode the streets. Getting through Venice Beach and Muscle Beach was always chaotic but exciting. My ears vibrated from the bass-booming, tricked-out El Camino low-riders.

We usually rode the Malibu mountains, which were surprisingly large. Some of the climbs were in excess of ten miles, with several thousand vertical feet of climbing. I was getting in huge volume and miles, but little intensity. And seven months of backpacking and beer drinking was not the best way to build a solid training base.

On one of these training rides, I had one of the worst crashes of my life. Dave was dropping off the back of the group and doing intervals on the climb to catch us. I thought it would be funny to give him a longer interval than he intended, so I went to the front of the group and began to push the pace. I went up and over the climb and continued to push at race pace on the descent. The descent was long and sinuous, and I pedaled hard through hairpin corners to maintain as much speed as I could. On one really tight corner I clipped my pedal on the pavement going about 30 miles an hour. The pedal strike threw my bike sideways and I wiped out hard. I smelled my flesh sear as I scraped along the blacktop, stopping just a few feet from a roadside drop-off. I was stranded 65 miles from home with an unrideable bike and road rash all over my body. My gloveless hands resembled freshly ground hamburger.

There was little traffic, but a group of kids who had ditched school to go to the beach passed by in a van. I flagged them down and they gave me a lift to the Point Mugu State Park. Park rangers had a small medical kit and patched me up a bit, but they thought I should go to the hospital to have the wounds cleaned properly. I didn't have money or health insurance, so I refused. I finally got through to my grandparents, and they picked me up and gave me a ride home to my dad's.

By the time I got home, I was really stiff and sore and my wounds were in bad shape. Lorraine was finishing up her degree at UCLA and also was staying at our dad's. Lorraine and I have always been close. She and I shuttled back and forth between Telluride and LA together. It was always the two of us. We are two sides of the same coin: I look like our mom, with our dad's coloring, and she looks like our dad, with our mom's coloring. I have always been there for Lorraine, and she has always been there for me. Right then, my skin sandpapered and swollen, I needed Lorraine more than ever.

My wounds needed cleaning to avoid infection, but it was too painful to do myself. I couldn't make myself scrub hard enough. I stripped off what was left of my shredded cycling kit, filled the bathtub, and lowered myself into the water, which stung my injuries anew. I convinced Lorraine to take a brush and scrub my wounds. I was in complete agony, grimacing as she methodically worked gravel out of my legs and arms. The water in the tub swirled crimson with blood. Lorraine was in tears. She was afraid she was going to injure me further. The brush couldn't dislodge the deepest debris, so Lorraine grabbed tweezers and plucked sticks and rocks out of my shoulders, elbows, and hips. She witnessed my pain and shame. Naked and bleeding in the bathtub, I was vulnerable and suffering.

That was a low point for me. I was flat broke, working as a bus boy, and getting my ass kicked in every race. I also felt incredibly weak and at 6 foot 3 weighed just 155 pounds. But I didn't want to quit. Despite the incredible odds, I had set a big goal. I had made up my mind to try out for the 1992 Olympic Team.

There were other obstacles. My dad and I were not getting along. He thought I was wasting my life — and my Berkeley education — and that I needed to grow up. He wanted me to go to business school or get a job at an investment bank. I thought those were pretty good options, too, but I wasn't ready to get a full time job and be tied down. Not yet. When Dad prodded me about what I wanted to do and I finally confessed I wanted to focus on training and try out for the Olympics, he couldn't hold back his frustration and disappointment any longer.

He came unglued.

"What are you talking about?" Dad exploded, exasperated. Even though I'd been formulating this plan for almost a year, to him it was out of the blue. And it was hardly the next logical step in establishing my own grownup life.

"Now you want to be a bicyclist?" he said, trying to connect the dots of my lurching career path. "You are going to the Olympics next year? Give me a break."

"I think I have a chance …" I started. He was having none of it. "We're in LA. You should just be a movie star. It pays better!" he snapped back.

I was tired of LA, tired of living with my dad, and tired of clearing people's dirty dishes. I loaded up the Yellow Bomber, crossed my fingers it would be mechanically sound enough to make the 900-mile journey inland, and drove home to Telluride to give cycling one last push. I really wanted to try and get my Cat. 1 upgrade and knew if I placed in the Top 20 at the National Championship road race I would automatically get an upgrade. In 1991 there were only about 120 Category 1 riders in the entire country. Thinking back, even that objective was ludicrous, to assume I could become one of the top riders in the country in just five months of racing and training.

When I got to Telluride, my mom took one look at me and was concerned about my low weight. She made me go see a doctor. Lab tests confirmed I had picked up a parasite in Asia. Medication cleared it up and I started to gain weight and strength again. During training, I regularly did intervals: lots of 2- to 3-minute hill repeats up the airport road until I would vomit.

To this day I'm not sure what was driving me so hard. I had never really excelled athletically, and I don't think I'm all that competitive. There was something inside me that would not let me quit — some sort of rage — rage at myself and the world. I was tired of being a loser. I wanted to prove my LA dad wrong, but it was more than that. The pain from the intervals was intense, but I wouldn't back off. I'd play these crazy mind games where I would scream at myself to keep going. I would get into a zone where it was almost an out-of-body experience — like I was detached, watching this guy on the bike spill his guts out.

It's hard to describe how your body feels after doing intervals. Most people just quit — the pain is too much. Everything hurts. Your arms are starved of oxygen, your heart is pounding at 200 beats per minute, you're panting like a dog, the lactic acid in your legs is on fire, your head is throbbing, and it feels like a knife is jabbed into your lower rib cage. But you keep turning the pedals, keep pushing forward as if a pack of hungry wolves is nipping at your heels.

The 1991 National Championships were held in early July at elevation in Park City, Utah. The time spent training in the mountains of Telluride was good for me. I started to find some form and was eager to see how I would stack up against the best amateurs in the country. It was a 108-mile circuit race with significant climbing. Halfway through the race, Lance Armstrong attacked on the climb. And right when he attacked, I flatted. Rather than wait for the neutral support vehicle, I rode the flat tire up the hill to the feed zone where Lee (still a Cat. 3, by the way) was offering nutritional and mechanical support. Lee did a quick wheel change, but I'd still lost two or three minutes and was dead last. My days as a cyclist, I was starting to realize, might be coming to an end after all. But I felt strong, so I kept riding.

The circuit was about eight miles long and hilly, but the main climb was maybe a mile and a half or so. Here's where luck was on my side: The climb was almost identical in length and grade to the airport road near Telluride where I trained. I went as hard as I could and when I got to the base of the climb I saw a half-dozen riders ahead of me. I did an interval on the climb and caught them. Each time I completed a circuit I'd see another small group of riders up the road for me to chase. I kept leapfrogging groups, and near the end of the race I'd bridged up to the main peloton.

I didn't know how many guys were still up the road, but I was in a group of some thirty riders. We were coming up to the finish line and with about a mile to go I attacked the group and finished by myself. That attack earned me fifteenth place on the day. I didn't know it at the time, but fifteenth place was significant, because the top 15 earned an automatic placement to the U.S. National B Team. Fifteenth place was the cutoff.

I did know, however, that with a Top 20 I had earned my Cat. 1 upgrade. After the finish I pressed Yvonne Van Gent, one of the officials I knew from Colorado, to sign my license for the upgrade.

She leveled a patient smile at me.

"It's okay, Scott. We will mail it to you. Good job," she said.

I was stoked. I had met my goal and was now convinced I needed to keep racing for another year. The Olympics were just thirteen months away.

Win True

Chapter 6
KNOCK ON OPPORTUNITY'S DOOR

Don't wait for opportunity to knock.
Go banging on doors.

Almost every major opportunity in my life has been as a result of my proactive efforts to make a change. For the next few months, I went banging on doors.

After my result in Park City, I knew I needed to learn how to handle a bike better and how to read a race better. USA Cycling periodically hosted camps for beginner riders who wanted to learn how to race. There were four categories in men's road and track racing, starting at 4 and ascending to 1. I signed up for a September Category 4 Camp at the Olympic Training Center in Colorado Springs. I was by far the strongest — but least experienced — rider there.

One of our training days involved learning how to position ourselves in the field during a criterium: a short, tight race of laps around a closed circuit. The coaches decided we would race a miss and out. A miss and out is a race on a circuit or a track where the last rider in the group at the start/finish line is eliminated. A rider is eliminated each lap until there are only two riders left. So, if you start with twenty riders, you'll end up completing nineteen laps.

The final two riders sprint for the win on the last lap. The coach was a racer, a Cat. 1, and he raced the miss and out with us. With ten to twelve laps to go, I was still in the group. It got aggressive. I fought for position and made the cut each lap, but just barely. Finally, it was just me and the coach: the last two riders. He was quick and experienced, and I was pretty sure he would beat me in a straight-up sprint. I needed to drop him before the end of the lap and finish alone. I attacked hard, got a gap, but went too hot into the last corner and crashed hard. I didn't win, but I definitely made a statement. I was strong, eager to learn, and not afraid.

One evening a new coach led a classroom session about racing tactics. It was Chris Carmichael, head coach of the U.S. Men's Road Team. I went over to Coach Carmichael after the meeting and talked to him about my goals of improving as a cyclist. I told him a bit of my story and how I had just started.

"What's your name?" Coach Carmichael asked.

"Scott Mercier," I answered.

That sparked his memory. "I remember you from Park City," he said. "We talked after the race, and you told me you hadn't been racing long. You're obviously a strong athlete, but you need to work on your bike-handling skills."

"That's why I'm here," I said.

"You have good endurance," Coach said. He'd obviously sized me up. "You have a big engine."

Coach Carmichael told me there was a National Team camp coming up in November that I was welcome to attend. That's what I mean about looking for opportunity; Coach never would have invited me if I hadn't shown some initiative.

There were probably thirty athletes invited to the November camp, including my friend Doug Loveday. Doug was a friend of Bobby Stuckey's and we'd all become friends from training together in Flagstaff. One day the coaches posted a list of the riders selected for the 1992 National Team. Doug and I leaned in and scanned the list for our names. He was behind me and couldn't see his name yet, but I could. I turned to him and said, "Lovedog, you made the National Team!" I was excited for him. The list was alphabetical, so

I continued to scan down the names and saw "Mercier, Scott."

I thought: *Holy shit. I'm on the National Team!* I couldn't believe it.

During the camp, an early winter snowstorm hit Colorado Springs. It was too cold and wet to train outside so the coaches decided we would have a water day and play around in the pool. "Hey, let's see how far you guys can swim underwater," one of the coaches challenged.

We might have thought this was a water "play" day, but play was the furthest thing from the coaches' minds. This was going to be a test. I now tell young athletes that if they are ever invited to the Olympic Training Center, they should be aware that everything the coaches have them do is a test. If athletes are invited to play ping-pong, it is a test of hand-eye coordination. If they are encouraged to swim underwater, it is a test of their lungs. There's no fun and games at the Olympic level. Everything is a test of some sort. While coaches might design an activity to look fun, they are actually watching you closely, evaluating your performance.

But we didn't know that. Surrounded by these elite athletes, my competitive drive kicked in. I swam almost a full length farther than anyone else. I think I did 2½ lengths and practically drowned myself. I surfaced, gasping and coughing. I pushed myself as far as I could go. The head soigneur for the national team, Charlie Livermore, noticed how far I swam.

Soigneurs provide a broad range of support to cycling teams — everything from washing laundry and arranging for meals and transportation to giving massages and offering moral support. Soigneur is a French term meaning "one who treats." Deeply embedded into every aspect of training and competition, soigneurs are the trusted eyes and ears of the team and the caretakers of the riders.

Charlie told Coach Carmichael: "You've got to check this kid out. He's got some big lungs."

After we toweled off, Charlie said to me, "You need to consider the team time trial because you've got big lungs and big power and it might be a good event for you."

I was down for anything. "Great! What's a team time trial?" I asked.

After a beat he responded, "You'll find out."

I didn't know it at the time, but the team time trial, or TTT, is perhaps the hardest event in cycling. The Olympic team time trial was a four-man, 100-kilometer race against the clock. The TTT is the equivalent of running wind sprints across a gym and then jogging back and immediately sprinting back — for two hours. You are on the rivet the entire time. The guy in the front of the team essentially does a sprint for 15 to 20 seconds and then gets back into the draft to recover for a minute before he sprints again. There are no breaks and the only water or food allowed is what you start with on your bike. So if it's really hot and you drink all your water too early, you're going to be extremely dehydrated, except you can't quit because you have two or three other guys relying on you.

With my raw talent — heavy emphasis on *raw* — Coach Carmichael thought I was a good fit for the grueling TTT.

"The event we have earmarked for you is the four-man team time trial," he told me.

He explained the strategy.

"The tactics for the team time trial are pretty simple: Get four big guys with huge engines that can just haul ass for 100 kilometers and go as hard as they can until they start to bleed from their eyeballs. It fits you really well."

Another day in camp, we all went cross-country skiing — now we were in my territory. I had grown up skiing, and these were a bunch of *cyclists*. I was determined to put the hurt on everybody, and I killed them. Even Coach Carmichael couldn't stay close. I was a hundred meters ahead and breaking the trail up a climb.

Coach screamed at me: "We're done! We're turning around!"

My performance at that fall camp got me invited to the next round of winter camps in January. These were smaller, cycling-focused, intense camps. I was starting to get noticed. At the end of the camp, Coach Carmichael gave me some training programs and said he wanted me to stay in touch.

"I'm planning a team time trial camp in the spring and I want you there," he told me.

I left Colorado Springs with significantly improved fitness and confidence. My tactical acumen was not very refined yet — I would say that on the stages of evolution I had progressed to Neanderthal — but I had power, could climb, and wasn't afraid to attack. I went to some big stage races in early 1992 and did really well. I was the top amateur in most of the races I entered.

The Tour of Bisbee in Arizona was one of the biggest stage races on the domestic calendar. One day I got in a breakaway and was outsprinted by Nathan Dahlberg. I placed second on the stage, was the top amateur, and finished eleventh overall. I still was stupid and didn't know how to race, but I knew that if you attack you put yourself in a position to win.

That spring I called Coach Carmichael.

"Hey, coach, this is Scott. I'm calling to follow up with you about the team time trial camp we discussed last fall. I'd like to go," I said. This was on a Friday or Saturday.

"It starts tomorrow! Get your ass down here!" he answered.

He probably hadn't even remembered that he'd invited me to a team time trial camp. If I hadn't taken the initiative and made that phone call, it's unlikely I would have been at the camp.

I was in Telluride, 300 miles and several mountain passes away. "I've got to go to Colorado Springs," I told my mom. "Can you take me down there?" As always, she came through. We got to the Olympic Training Center and there were twelve riders at the camp. The head coach of USA Cycling, Jiri Mainus, a Czech, was running the camp.

We all found a seat in a small conference room for the first meeting. Coach Mainus ran through the rules of the camp, including diet and curfew, and laid out the type of training we would do specific to the team time trial.

Then, totally unexpected to me, he announced: "This is the Olympic Long Team Camp. Of the twelve of you in this room, four of you will be going to the Olympic Games."

I had never even done a team time trial. I looked around at the other riders and thought, *I have a one-in-three chance of making the Olympic team.* I couldn't believe it. I still get goosebumps thinking about it. Until that moment, I had no idea the camp was connected to the Olympics. I use that moment as a life lesson when I speak to young athletes: You have to proactively look for opportunity. There were other guys good enough to be there, but they were not proactive enough. I had made it known that I wanted to learn; I wanted to be good.

Coach Mainus finished speaking and one of the riders on the National A team, turned to me and said: "No way will you make the Olympic Team. They are using you for training fodder, but you might have a chance to make the World Championship Team in 1993."

It really pissed me off, quite frankly. I thought to myself, *Training fodder? Screw you. You are training fodder!*

So there I was. It was April of 1992, and I was on the Long Team for the Olympics. We did a ton of painful workouts, but the motor-pacing sessions and pace lines are particularly memorable. Motor-pacing is a crazy exercise where riders draft behind a motorcycle. The training simulates race speeds and is exceptionally hard because of the fact that the motorcycle doesn't get tired. The driver puts the motorcycle in third or fourth gear so that it isn't too punchy. The motorcycle gradually slows on the climbs and gradually accelerates on the descents. Attached to the back of the motorcycle is a roller, which is a safety device designed to keep cyclists from hitting the motorcycle and crashing if they get too close.

When we were going slower a lot of the riders would hit the roller with their front wheel on purpose. You take your front wheel and jam it into the roller and it spins. We used it for bike-handling skills. The coaches didn't encourage it, but we did it anyway. So you're going 30 miles an hour and you strike the roller, and it makes a loud whizzing sound. I was terrified at first, but I wasn't going to let my competitors think I was a wimp. Thank God nobody crashed; it would have been horrible.

We turned it into a game where you hit the roller with so much speed you bounce off it. Since it would spin it wouldn't lock up your front tire. It was really freaking stupid, actually, but fun, too. We did most of our motor-pacing over the rolling terrain of the Black Hills, east of Colorado Springs.

A twelve-man motor-pacing session is ridiculously difficult and chaotic. Right behind the motorcycle is the most draft. But you don't get to hang out behind the motorcycle. You're there for 5 to 10 seconds, then you're supposed to pull off and let the next person in. Once you pull off, you lose the draft and get hit with a wall of wind. Your speed drops precipitously and you drift toward the back of the line of riders. By the time you're near the back your speed has dropped by 8 to 10 miles an hour and you have to sprint as hard as you can to catch the last guy's wheel so you don't get dropped.

With twelve riders the last guy is some 70 feet behind the motorcycle. You're riding along with this string of riders and the motorcycle is going 30 to 35 miles an hour. Inevitably someone will blow. It's not usually the guy at the back who blows but rather the rider in sixth or seventh position. When he blows it creates an instant gap between the riders in front of him and the riders behind him; the blown rider's speed will almost instantly slow by 10 to 15 miles an hour. When you blow in efforts like these, you've typically gone so far into the red that you can't pedal anymore. If you're behind this rider, you have to make a Herculean effort to get back to the front group. You've got to sprint as hard as you can to close a 30- to 40-foot gap and get back in the draft.

I'd never motor-paced before, but I knew the workouts were important and I needed to distinguish myself. I made a vow I'd never get dropped from the line. If someone blew ahead of me, I was going to close the gap. When guys start blowing, it's really important to pay attention to what's happening in front of you. You're usually going so hard you can barely see straight, but if you don't look up the road you're going to get gapped off.

Every single time I was the last guy to stay with the motorcycle; everybody else would blow. Coach Mainus would keep going for another 3 or 4 miles. I'm not sure if he knew it or not, but I was always on the verge of blowing when he would slow down to let the other riders catch up.

One day he eased up and spoke to me directly for the first time.

"Where the hell have you been the last few years?" he interrogated in his heavy Eastern European accent.

"I've been in college, ski racing, drinking beer, and backpacking!" I replied.

Coach just shook his head.

Another training tactic we used was called the pace line. Pace line training is also extremely hard. Pace line training is designed to mimic the team time trial by forcing riders to stay together as a group at speed. Riders form two parallel lines, windward and leeward, and take turns at the front of the windward line for 10 to 15 seconds, breaking the wind then moving over to the leeward line for a slight recovery. The rotation of the two lines forms a forward elliptical movement.

It was important for the team to stay together because more riders are faster than fewer riders, just as with a peloton. We usually were broken into two groups of six for the pace line exercises. The coaches rode motorcycles next to us so they could see what was going on and give instructions. Most of the time the instructions were to try to catch the group of six in front or drop the group of six behind, thus turning it into a race.

These training exercises were usually done on rolling hills, as well. The goal was to keep the six riders together as a group for as long as possible. Eventually, guys would start to get dropped on the climbs, and when I'd see this I'd put my hand on their lower back and physically push them back into the draft of the rider ahead, keeping the pace line intact. I did this for two reasons: to keep the group together as the coaches had instructed and to show I was the strongest guy there — strong enough not just to hang with the group, but to push weaker riders up the hills as well. I wanted to make a statement. It was like cycling's version of counting coup. I was determined to prove I wasn't training fodder.

The coaches watched all of this. They saw guys blow, and they saw a kid who'd never done one of these events make the cut every time. On top of that, this kid was shoving other guys forward so they wouldn't get dropped, so the pace line didn't get blown out.

I know that pissed off a lot of the other riders because there was supposed to be a natural pecking order, a hierarchy based on tenure and experience, but I didn't care. I had no friends at this camp. I was an outsider, the enemy, and I was becoming a significant threat to someone's spot on the Olympic Team. I was there to race. I was there to take my opportunity to represent Team USA in Barcelona.

In the world of sports, nothing is a given birthright; it's all earned. By the time the camp ended in late May, I had muscled my way onto the A Squad for the National Championships, which also served as the Olympic Trials.

To be Olympians, though, we still had to race.

And we had to win.

Win True

Chapter 7

SPEAK YOUR MIND

If you have something to say, say it.
Always argue your case.

The Olympic Trials were open to any teams, and about twenty-five squads were entered. USA Cycling entered both our A and B Squads. We still had to win the Olympic Trials at Nationals to solidify our spot on the four-man team time trial Olympic team. The only reason the coaches had opened up the competition to the long team in the first place was because the guys they initially wanted on the team were getting their asses kicked racing the spring season in Europe. The coaches wanted to recruit some new athletes. I was the only new athlete to make the cut, so I had a lot to prove.

We competed in some of the biggest stage races — which are over multiple days — in America. I didn't finish in the Top 20, but I was the top amateur at the Tour of West Virginia. Darren Baker took third in the Thrift Drug Classic in Pittsburgh, which Lance Armstrong won. I was the only other guy from the team who finished in Pittsburgh, and I think I finished about 24th. Then we went to Altoona, Pennsylvania, for the Olympic Trials. I still had never done a 100-kilometer, four-man team time trial.

There was open animosity from some of the other riders towards me. I mean here I was, a guy who came from nowhere, and I was

65

selected for the Olympic Long Team. The four-man team was George Hincapie, Dave Nicholson, Nate Sheafor, and me.

The race was a rolling course of 100 kilometers, and it was hot and humid. Nate's strategy was that we would start at a conservative, but fast pace and hold that pace for 100 kilometers, with the thought that the other teams would come back to us, which is exactly what happened.

We started at a steady pace, but at the 25-kilometer mark Nate flatted and we were about 1½ minutes down. We didn't panic but kept rolling along at a steady pace with everyone riding strong and sharing the workload. At the 50-kilometer mark we had cut into our deficit and were about a minute down, maybe less. At the 75-kilometer mark we were in the lead and we knew we were going to win the race, but we still had 25 kilometers to go.

Stifling heat and blanketing humidity took its toll on my clear-mountain-air-trained body. The sweat clung; it felt like there was more water outside of me than inside. My stomach revolted and flipped. *Damn it!* I thought. *If we win this race, all four of us together, we will all be going to Barcelona. If the rest of the team wins this race but I get dropped, those three will be in, but I won't be going.* I knew I could not miss a turn at the front. I could not show any weakness. I absolutely could not get dropped.

I could still control my legs, but my stomach defied my resolve and I started puking, heaving in spasms. I was so scared my coaches and teammates would see I was sick and weak that my mouth and cheeks filled with vomit and I forced myself to swallow it back down rather than spew it out for all to see. That's how badly I wanted to win: I swallowed my own puke. Fortunately, I had a little water left to wash the puke down. Nobody knew I had thrown up — not my teammates, not my coaches. I never told anyone.

Propelled by anger at myself for getting sick, on my next turn on the front I nearly dropped the team. It was the last big climb of the race and I was trying to rip my legs off. "Ease up!" the team yelled at me. We powered toward the finish line and the team mechanic poked out the sunroof in the support car behind us and hoisted a bullhorn. His enthusiasm was amplified: "You are National Champions and you're going to Barcelona!"

Crossing the finish line was one of the greatest feelings of my life. I wasn't alone in my celebration. I got to share it with my Telluride dad, who comprised my family cheering section for this race. Dad had purchased $1,200 binoculars so he could follow me as much as possible on the course. I focused on him as I crossed the line, those expensive binoculars around his neck and his face beaming with pride. I knew I wouldn't have been there if it hadn't been for him.

I felt a sense of validation. In the individual time trial I'd placed only 19th. I knew other riders didn't think I belonged in their ranks, and I'd proved I did. Not only had we won, but I'd also proven to be the strongest guy on the team that day. In just sixteen months since starting my racing career, I went from zero to the Olympic Games. It was a fast climb, and it was the combination of me looking for the opportunity, wanting it more than anybody else, and some of the chosen ones falling on their faces.

After the Olympic Trials we all went home for a week. I was the first Olympian to come out of Telluride. It was a pretty big deal for my friends and family. My parents threw a huge party at their home. Dad was a volunteer fireman, and a couple of guys went down to the fire station and drove back an enormous, bright-red fire truck. Eventually, several of us decided we were going to parade this fire truck around town.

We'd all had quite a few cold beers at that point. My mom had a flag, so I was waving the U.S. flag and there must have been fifty of us who piled on the truck. We drove around town with the sirens blaring and signs on the side that read, "We are going to Barcelona!" It all was totally impromptu and small-town America — Norman Rockwell, lubricated with Coors.

Our celebratory parade ended up at the base of Imogene Pass on Tomboy Road. We parked the fire truck in the middle of the road and lit off fireworks. The cops came and told us to move the fire truck because emergency responders couldn't get through if there was a call.

"Emergency responders? one of Dad's friends piped up. "We've got the fire department right here!"

From Telluride I traveled to Florida, where all U.S. Olympians went through a processing center to receive their official clothing, shoes, swag, and credentials. Picture a Costco with shelves and racks stocked with nothing but red-white-and-blue. George and I went through processing together, pushing big shopping carts and heaping on our logoed gear. A Ralph Lauren tailor fit us for our opening ceremonies uniforms. A cobbler fit us for shoes. There were jean jackets embroidered with American flags, Olympic-branded sunglasses, socks, shorts, and cellophane bags of trading pins. Every Olympian received thousands of dollars' worth of high-end wardrobing for Barcelona, much of it with our name and the Barcelona '92 Olympics logo. We were dressed for American success.

My celebration as a laurel-crowned Olympian, however, was short-lived. My seemingly limitless soar as a cyclist took a hard downward turn — tumbling Icarus of the melted-wax wings, landing on the point of an Official Olympics Trading Pin.

Disaster started to strike once the team got to Spain. The first calamity took out our captain, our rock, Dave Nicholson. Dave was so damn strong and steady. This guy could ride at 31 miles an hour for a long time. He was a tough SOB. Dave was out by himself on a training ride and was nearly hit by a car. He swerved to avoid the vehicle, skidded in gravel, and broke the socket of his hip right where it goes into the femur. That was just a week before the Olympics. The loss of our captain felt insurmountable. It shook our team.

We were still rooming out of town and hadn't even gone to the Olympic Village yet. We brought over our alternate, John Stenner, who also was a beast of a man. John was the reigning national champion in the individual time trial. None of the alternates had trained with the four of us in Colorado Springs, including John.

That was the first mistake.

The day of the Olympic Games, Coach Carmichael and Nate, our new captain, laid out the strategy to the team. It would be a repeat of the approach that had worked so well at Nationals. But at Nationals, we'd raced against the best the U.S. had to offer. Now we were racing against the best in the world.

"We're going to start steady and finish steady," coach said.

I was taken aback. *We'd fought to get here. That's what had worked!* This approach felt wrong. It went against my instincts. *Steady?* I thought. *I'd rather fight for the win!*

I wish I would have spoken up — cautious and checked was not the way I wanted to ride. I wanted to start hard and if we blew, then we blew. It was the Olympic Games and I didn't want to ride for eighth place. Only three teams would make the podium. I wanted to be in the mix. But I was the new guy and I'd only done one event, so I didn't speak up. That was one of my biggest regrets in cycling, that I didn't speak out against a bad strategy. I wanted to go balls out, and if we went down, at least we went down fighting. Plus, when you're fighting for a podium spot, you can often mentally find that extra one or two percent and keep suffering.

The team time trial was the first event, the kickoff to the Olympic Games on July 26, which meant we did not get to participate in the opening ceremonies because we couldn't be on our feet for six hours the day before the race. My whole family came to Barcelona to support me. They enjoyed the opening ceremonies — where archer Antonio Rebollo dramatically lit the Olympic cauldron with a flaming arrow — then they lined up to watch my one shot at Olympic glory the next morning.

On race day, the team warmed up on trainers in the stadium. I spotted the spare bikes on the team car. They had just one water bottle each.

"Shouldn't they have two water bottles?" I asked Coach Carmichael.

"No, we won't need them," he said, meaning the spare bikes.

That didn't make any sense to me. Why even have spare bikes if you don't have them fully outfitted to ride?

No matter. It was go-time. Barely 10 kilometers into the race we hit two massive potholes before the first turnaround, and George flatted. We all stopped to wait for him to have a wheel change. Then he flatted again! After that, George felt there was something wrong with the bike so we stopped again for a bike change.

We weren't even at the first turn, we were 12 kilometers into the race, and we'd already had mechanical failures and a bike change. This threw us off our game immediately. It was 90-plus degrees and 90 percent humidity. The route was four 25-kilometer laps and we were near the first turnaround when the French team passed us. They'd started 3 minutes behind us. Nate's strategy was to keep going steady. Fifty kilometers into the race George ran out of water because of the single water bottle on his spare bike. At 55 kilometers he was off the back. We were down to three guys, and we had to finish with three.

By the 65-kilometer mark, Nate was blown and we basically had to drag him to the finish line with John and me doing all the work. Nate was sitting on — too tired to take his turn in front — and he couldn't even hold the wheel, so we had to keep waiting for him. There was one climb on the circuit of about a kilometer. It wasn't that steep, and we normally would have charged up the hill in the big ring at 18 to 20 miles an hour, but Nate was suffering and we slowed to about 12 miles an hour in the small-chain ring. *Steady my ass,* I thought. I was sitting on the tops of the bars, out of the aerodynamic time trial position. Normally you'd never get out of your time trial bars, but I was on the hoods, just like I'd be on a training ride. John was at the front and I was monitoring Nate. At that point we were soft-pedaling. We limped across the finish line with a time of 2 hours, 13 minutes. We were about 15 minutes slower than our National Championship time. We finished in fucking sixteenth place. We got to the line and John and I weren't even tired. We were like: *Can we have a Mulligan? Can we do that over?* Obviously, there are no Mulligans in the Olympic Games.

To this day our performance at the Olympics remains one of the most humiliating and disappointing days in my life. If we'd just ridden our time from the Nationals we would have finished in the Top 5. The courses and conditions were almost identical, and we'd even been slowed by a mechanical failure in Altoona, too. I believe in my heart that we should have finished in third to seventh place. More than medaling, I just wanted to get to the finish line of the Olympic Games knowing we'd done everything we possibly could as an Olympic team. We didn't. We finished with our tail between our red-white-and-blue-wrapped legs.

The entire U.S. Olympic cycling team came home with just one medal; it was an unmitigated disaster. In the team time trial, there were really only about fifteen competitive teams. The Chinese beat us; they were fifteenth. We'd beaten the Swedes, but they had more problems than we had. I think we beat Iran. I could find the results again, but I don't like to think about it too much. 1992 was the last time the team time trial was competed at the Olympic Games. The International Olympic Committee only gives so many spots to cycling, and the team time trial was dropped to make room for up-and-coming mountain biking.

Here's what else I learned: If you have something to say, say it. People might not agree with it, but always argue your case. I learned a lot about leadership, too — particularly what not to do. And I learned you should always prepare for the unexpected. We didn't do any of that with the alternates, the water bottles, and the new and untested equipment. You never should change anything on race day. If you hear about some newfangled food, never eat it on race day. Try everything in training first. We never even trained what to do if we lost a team member.

John and I roomed together in the Olympic Village after the team time trial. After our humiliating loss, I was depressed and angry for probably six hours — I couldn't talk to anyone. Then I thought, *It is only the first day of the Olympics, and I am going to have a good time through the rest of it.* I shifted gears from athlete to fan and didn't touch my bike again in Barcelona.

As Olympians, you get a lot of free tickets, but if you want to guarantee a seat at certain events you need to buy them. You get first dibs from a list. Now a full-on fan, I went down the list, checking all the events I thought my family might want to see — I was just checking off almost everything. I gave the completed list to my Telluride dad, thinking he would narrow it down. He didn't change anything. When he got to the ticket counter, the total was almost $5,000. It was a lot of money. He hesitated but paid it. *"When am I going to go to the Olympics again?"* he reasoned. My whole family was all in to live in the moment.

We attended a lot of events: gymnastics, diving, swimming, tennis. My favorite was boxing — especially if the match had one of the African fighters. The atmosphere was exhilarating, with teammates banging on African drums. If it was just a preliminary match, you could be as close as 20 feet from the action in the ring, pulsing in percussive unison with the boxers, their teammates, and the crowd.

1992 also marked the return to the Summer Olympics for South Africa, since being banned in 1963 for its apartheid policy. There was much for the world to celebrate.

Barcelona with its beaches and nightclubs was an unbelievably fun place — even more so if you had Olympic credentials dangling around your neck. I partied with my sister and former racing buddy Doug Alvaredo. We'd get to the clubs and there'd be people waiting in line for two hours to get in. Bouncers would spot an Olympic athlete in line and — boom! — we were ushered in like VIPs.

Bouncers didn't care if you were competing in fencing, cycling, or badminton. All Olympians got treated like rock stars. It was also the year of the first Dream Team, so when it came to American athletes, club owners really were hoping for brash basketball power forward Charles Barkley, whose larger-than-life star-power could fill the place. In one club I finagled my way behind the bar and mixed cocktails and poured sangrias until 3 in the morning. The music was cranking, and we danced and laughed until we were exhausted. Once I decided I was going to fully enjoy the Olympics, I saw a lot of sunrises, and not from getting up early.

There was racing success after the crushing loss at the Olympics. I finished the year placing pretty well in two of the bigger stage races in the U.S. at the time: Celestial Seasonings Classic in Colorado and the Killington Stage Race in Vermont. I had just completed my second full year of racing and had two offers from professional teams, and Coach Carmichael wanted me to stay with the National Team for another year.

My burning ambition, however, was to turn pro and race in Europe. I had watched Greg LeMond beat Laurent Fignon in the 1989 Tour de France while I was a junior at Cal. Witnessing LeMond's success made it seem possible for me. I chose the Saturn Cycling Team because Team Director Warren Gibson had big plans and said he was going to take us to Europe, which is the major leagues for cycling.

I negotiated a contract of $2,000 a month and I felt like I was in heaven. I was getting paid to travel and race my bike. What more could I ask for?

Win True

Chapter 8
LOSE AND LEARN

*Success is being a little bit better, a little bit smarter,
and a little bit stronger every day.*

Saturn's Team Director Warren Gibson, affectionately known as Gibbo, was a good friend of Greg Lemond. At least according to Gibbo they were. In 1991, Lemond had completed a training ride down Mexico's Baja Peninsula to help him prepare for the upcoming European season. Gibbo thought that was a great idea, so he planned our first training camp to be a 1,000-mile ride from Ensenada to Cabo along Mexican Highway 1.

The team met in San Diego and got fitted for our new bikes and kits. We had several sponsors and members of the cycling media join us, so our total group was around twenty-five.

I really couldn't believe I was getting a paycheck to do something like this. The Team Saturn training camp promised to be as much an adventure as a cycling camp. I was less than two years removed from living out of a backpack in hostels around Southeast Asia, so the thought of riding a bike along the Cabo coast was thrilling.

We drove ten miles south of Ensenada and unloaded our bikes. Gibbo broke us into small groups of two to three riders with a sponsor or member of the media. We were going to ride upwards of 80-100 miles a day. This was early January, and most of us were neo-pros who hadn't been training much. The sponsors and media members, however, treated this like it was the World Championship.

My group consisted of Scott Fortner, Dave McCook, and a journalist from *Bicycling* magazine. In 1993, Highway 1 was a narrow, two-lane road, littered with broken glass and cavernous pot-holes. Gibbo had a support car behind each group driven by a mechanic or soigneur to provide protection from the traffic.

The spine of the Baja Peninsula is mountainous, and even though we were skirting the coast, the road is an undulating series of climbs and descents. The journalist in our group was fit. He half-wheeled all of us, and by the end of the first day we were irritated and tired.

Day Two greeted us with gray skies and pouring rain. We saddled up and continued our southern migration. It's surprising how cold and stinging a winter desert rain can be. We had 100 miles to ride in a downpour. Rainfall in the desert also tends to lead to flooding, as the hard ground with minimal vegetation doesn't absorb moisture quickly. As the rain continued, the arroyos started to run with water. The Mexican roads, at this time at least, just went up and down the arroyos, with very few bridges or drainages. At first the water was only two to three inches deep and we had no trouble riding through it.

Toward the end of the day, however, we came across an impassable arroyo. It was flooded with three feet of roiling, chocolate-milk-colored water and bobbing debris. We were close to our night's destination — so close that we could actually see the roadside motel on the other side of the rising water. Most of the mechanics and soigneurs had driven ahead to get the rooms and meals ready, so there were very few vehicles left behind where we could find shelter from the elements. Traffic was backed up and we stood on the side of the road, soaking wet and shivering.

About fifteen minutes passed before we heard a loud honking from one of the big rigs carrying supplies and goods to be trucked south to Cabo resorts. He was going for it. The driver accelerated into the rushing water. It filled his wheel wells and billowed and split as alongside the bow of a freighter. For the full eighty feet the truck parted the murky waters. We cheered: He made it!

This emboldened other idling truckers that they could make it, too. As the next truck approached, Gibbo stepped in front and waved it to a stop. He told the driver, "I've got a hundred bucks if you can take three of my riders across the water to that motel right there."

We climbed into the truck and anxiously clung to the door and dashboard as the truck plowed through churning water. It cost Gibbo about $500 to get the entire team across.

After watching the semis' successful voyages, our mechanic, Jeff, believed he could ford in one of the Saturn wagons. He steered to the far upstream edge of the road and gingerly started advancing. The water quickly rose to the windshield. Amazingly, the wagon didn't stall out. By the time Jeff got to the other side, he'd been washed significantly downstream. It was definitely not the smartest move, but it was amazing what those little cars could do.

The next day dawned clear and sunny. There was barely a trace of rainwater. We continued to pedal south. Several riders, however, developed knee pain and had to ride in team cars. Doing six-hour days right out of the chute probably wasn't the wisest of training techniques. At least three athletes developed such bad knee issues that they required surgery.

On the fifth or sixth day just north of Mulege, Jeff, our mechanic and truck driver, drifted to the side of the road and as he corrected to get back on the highway the truck toppled on its side. All of our spare bikes, wheels, clothing, food, etc., was in that truck. Everything we needed for the team and the camp lay rolled Over on Highway 1.

Gibbo wasn't sure what to do. He extended our stay in Mulege until he could figure out a plan. We still had about 400 miles of riding to get to Cabo.

Mulege is where we really bonded as a team via fermentation. We were stuck in a cramped motel in a small coastal town and had the added concern that the accident threatened the financial viability of the team. But what could we do? One night we just said *Fuck it* and enthusiastically patroned the only bar in town. I'm not sure what happened, as I was blackout drunk, but the good news is none of us got arrested. Scott Fortner, however, earned himself the nickname of Otis, as in the town drunk in *Mayberry*. He's one of my best friends, and we still call him Otis. Even riders from other teams call him Otis.

There was only one road in Mulege: Mexican Highway 1, so we could ride either north or south for our training rides. The ride south was spectacular. The road carved into a cliff several hundred feet above Bahia Concepcion (Conception Bay) and the contrast in color between the rusty desert and the turquoise water was striking. I've never been back, but I'd like to spend a week or so driving the peninsula. My mom and Telluride dad were snowbirds, and they made the drive from Telluride to Todos Santos for many years.

Eventually, somehow, Gibbo figured out a way to get us home, and we made final preparations for the upcoming season.

Europe, however, was no longer in the cards. It was going to be an expensive endeavor to race the spring campaign in Europe, and Saturn rejected the idea. Gibbo may have wanted the team to go to Europe, but he didn't have approval from the people signing the checks.

Instead, our first race was the Tour of Mexico. It was a big race, a fifteen-day stage race. The number-one team in the world was there, which at that time was the Gatorade Team. Their team was co-headlined by Gianni Bugno, the reigning World Champion, and Laurent Fignon, a winner of two Tours de France. There were some other big named riders as well. Raúl Alcalá was the most famous Mexican rider at the time — he was damn good. He rode for the Novell team and had won the biggest races in America, including the Coors Classic and the Tour DuPont. He had also won two stages of the Tour de France.

I'd just turned 25, and I was green and it showed. I wasn't aware at the time, but I still didn't know how to handle a bike very well. In fact, I ended up crashing three times during the Tour of Mexico. Tactically I wasn't very smart, either, because I hadn't been racing long. I had raced only half a season in 1991, so 1992 was my first full season. My first race as a professional would be a daunting fifteen-day stage race with a World Champion and a two-time Tour de France winner. The race would prove to be a pretty big introduction to professional racing and both the grueling physical and mental toughness required.

One of the first stages consisted of rolling hills and wind. The wind howled relentlessly. As a neophyte with little experience riding in the wind, this was a difficult day, to say the least.

Later on I became very effective in the wind and grew to love it because it played to my size and power. However, that day was humbling. A cross-wind, where the wind is coming from the side of the peloton rather than the front or rear, is one of the most feared phenomena in professional cycling. It splits the peloton like shrapnel because as guys stack up across the road seeking protection from the cross-wind, the confining width of the road eventually forces someone on the outside in the gutter, and that is not a good place to be.

When you're in the peloton in a cross-wind, instead of drafting behind, the shelter comes from the leeward side, so you're almost at a 45-degree angle. You're still riding your bike straight, but you'll ride next to the guy on the front, with your front wheel near the guy's handlebars; this is where you get the most shelter from the wind and the best draft. The guy behind you will have his front wheel near your handlebars, and on down the line. This is called an echelon. What makes these conditions so difficult is that the road is only so wide. You can't be stacked up riding next to riders for 100 yards across because the road isn't wide enough and someone ends up in the gutter. There is no draft at all in the gutter and the guys in front of you are all working together and getting rest in the draft. There is only room on the road for twenty to twenty-five riders.

To keep the echelon from getting too big, there is a usually a gatekeeper. The gatekeeper is the last guy in the line. He won't rotate through with the other guys, but rather his job is to keep everyone else out. If you are behind the gatekeeper then you are in the gutter.

Somehow I made the front group, but I didn't know what I was doing so they only let me go through a few rotations before the gatekeeper got in front of me and put me in the gutter. I hung on for dear life. I maybe made it three or four minutes before I got popped out.

Farther back there was another echelon, then another. This was a 192-rider field. After I got popped out of the first group I made the second. These were all pros. I was one of maybe two rookies in the group. The second echelon, same thing. I didn't know how to ride in the wind so I wasn't helping, the gatekeeper didn't want me in the echelon, so I got popped out again.

Eventually I was riding by myself. I think there was only one teammate who made one of the front echelons. The rest of us were screwed — cast out to struggle against the wind on our own. By the time I reached the finish line I had lost a huge chunk of time — maybe 20 minutes — but it was a long race and I had time to make up for earlier mistakes.

Still tactically naïve, I did at least know that by attacking you could put yourself in a position to win: a primal option. A few days later, undeterred by my shellacking in the cross-winds, I attacked. I got a decent gap but soon realized a Spanish rider had followed me. *Okay,* I thought. *I guess we're working as a team.* But the Spaniard sat on my wheel the entire time and did not contribute to our efforts one little bit. *Fucking freeloader!* We had a gap of probably 3 minutes and still he refused to work. I was doing all the work and he was getting all the benefits! *That's not the way it's supposed to work! There's reciprocity; you scratch my back, I scratch yours, right?!* I started getting worked up and began to lose my temper.

Time out: Before I confess my dumb-ass move, allow me a brief explanation. Years before I had watched *American Flyers,* the 1985 Kevin Costner movie about two brothers who work through sibling rivalry by training together for a grueling road race in Colorado. In the movie the race is called the Hell in the West, but it was based on the real-life Coors Classic that wended through the towering canyonlands of Colorado National Monument, where I'd once competed. At that easily influenced time in my young racing career, I was even taking racing tactics from Costner's overly mustachioed film character.

In celluloid drama, Costner sought to get rid of a "wheel suck," same as this freeloading Spaniard on my wheel, by swerving baaaack and foooorth across the road. I quickly determined this might also be the best tactic for me. After yelling at the guy — the wheel suck — and still not getting any help, I swerved wildly back and forth across the road and sprinted, then slowed down to try and get him off my wheel. Still, he stuck like glue. Finally, I hit the brakes and then sped ahead to try and get rid of him.

He finally had enough of my antics and sat up to join the chasing peloton. Needless to say, not only were my tactics incredibly stupid, but they were also dangerous. I could have caused him to crash and injure himself.

Once I was on my own, however, I put my head down and rode as hard as I could. My time gap held steady, but as we approached the finish line it began to tumble. The stage had a significant climb about 50 kilometers from the finish and my new goal became to get over the climb before the peloton caught me. Again, my tactics proved to be less than ideal. Once it was apparent that I would be caught, I continued to fight and to ride as hard as possible, rather than easing up so I could have some energy in reserve when I got caught. Gibbo drove up beside me and proffered tactical direction.

"When the peloton catches you, just stay with Fignon," he growled in his gravelly voice.

I could not believe it. Fignon was leading the race and had won the Tour de France. Twice! There was no way I was going to be able to stay with Fignon. I went crazy.

"Stay with Fignon?" I started yelling at him. "I'm going to be fucking lucky to stay with the group!"

I'll never forget that: "Stay with Fignon."

Several minutes later, the peloton caught me and they briefly eased up to give me some well-deserved grief. All the Spanish and Italian speaking riders started clapping and yelling, "Bravisimo!

Bravo! Fuerte! Championisimo!" This, of course, was due to my foolish tactics of trying to get rid of the Spanish rider who had been in the breakaway with me. I literally felt like I was two-years-old. It was a complete, but well deserved, smackdown. I was so green and so stupid. To this day I am both ashamed and embarrassed of my actions. However, I did make it over the last climb and was able to finish with the group and did not lose any more time.

Weird and unexpected things happen on the open roads of races. Early in the race a stray dog ran into the peloton and caused a huge crash. With international stars like reigning World Champion Gianni Bugno and Laurent Fignon in the field, this was an embarrassment for the hosting Mexicans. The Federales made sure this wouldn't happen again. We were informed that any unattended dogs on the side of the road would be shot by officers in the lead vehicles ahead of the race. I'm not sure if this was true, but we didn't have any other incidents with dogs.

On the fifth stage, tragedy struck. A drunk driver evaded the road closures and weaved onto the road and barreled straight toward the peloton. A brave and alert Federale in front of the race saw the truck heading toward the riders and rammed into the side of the truck to force it off the road. He probably saved dozens of lives. The truck slid onto the shoulder and the driver corrected back onto the road, slamming into the front third of the peloton. Riders flew into the air and dozens hit the ground. The drunk driver jammed the truck into reverse to get off the roadway and rammed into a press van. He pinned three riders to the van, including my teammate Clark Sheehan. Clark had won the prologue and was our best-placed and most-experienced rider. He broke three vertebrae and the accident nearly ended his career. After the crash there was mass confusion and anger. There were screams of agony and pools of blood on the road. Riders grabbed the driver of the truck and beat him senseless. This accident, thankfully, I avoided.

Each day I got a little bit better, a little bit smarter, and a little bit stronger. I slowly clawed my way up the general classification standings. The second-to-last stage of the Tour of Mexico was a massive pull. We climbed up the shoulder of the Iztaccihuatl Volcano on the outskirts of Mexico City. The dormant volcano is over 17,000 feet high. I was nervous, but I also knew it was a big opportunity for me and that I could move up in the standings if I could stay with the front group on the climb.

The day began with flat sunshine — a David Hockney sky. As the road ascended, I held with the front group. Riders got spit out the back right and left and before long the front group was down to fifteen riders. I finally could no longer hold the aggressive pace, but I managed to pace myself and not blow. I kept a steady, grinding tempo and by the time the race finished, I had moved up to eleventh overall.

For doping perspective, I think the field was relatively clean. It would not have been strategic for riders to have been amped-up on EPO for this race. There might have been some steroids and things like that to recover, but doping decisions weigh risk and reward. An early-season race in Mexico was as much a training race as anything. As I think back, it's fairly remarkable that in my first race as a professional, a fifteen- day stage race, I finished eleventh overall, racing against the reigning World Champion and two-time Tour de France champion. And that was despite my being a total bonehead and barely even knowing how to handle my bike. The Tour of Mexico was the last professional win for Laurent Fignon.

The prize money was supposed to go to twenty-five places, but the promoters didn't have enough money to pay out the full purse, so they decided to only pay the top 10. Because I finished eleventh, we made no prize money in that race. It was more than a bit shady and frustrating for us to have worked so hard and then get the shaft. So much for a Hollywood ending.

Back on home turf, the Tour DuPont was the biggest race in America and the Yanks' answer to the Tour de France. A spring, twelve-day race, it was sponsored by DuPont chemical company from 1991 to 1996 and attracted top European teams. The race started in Wilmington, Delaware, where DuPont is headquartered, and wound throughout the Mid-Atlantic States — North Carolina,

South Carolina, and Virginia — of the Blue Ridge Mountains.

Erik Breukink of the Netherlands won the first year. Greg LeMond won to host-country fanfare in 1992. The 1993 Tour DuPont was my first attempt at the race and my result was an important one for me: I won King of the Mountains, which was much-needed affirmation in my young career. The overall winner that year was Raúl Alcalá of Mexico. Lance Armstrong took second, launching his star as an up-and-coming cyclist. Future Postal teammate Viatcheslav Ekimov of Russia won in 1994, and Lance went on to win back-to-back in 1995 and 1996.

There were three big jerseys: the overall winner, the mountain winner, and the sprint winner. In 1993 Lance had just signed with Motorola and actually played a role in my win. There was a tight competition between me and a Spanish kid named Jose Manuel Uría. He was a little guy, a climber, and we were battling it out for the King of the Mountains.

On the fifth or sixth stage, we were climbing hard and fighting for position some 500 meters or so from the sprint line. I was sort of in the gutter, and one of Uría's teammates knocked me off the road — he came from the right and rode into me with his shoulder. I didn't crash, but I was literally off the side of the road in the dirt. My teammate Brian Walton saw this, so of course what did he do? He took their guy Uría off the road. Brian was a little guy, too, but he knew how the game was played. It's sort of like baseball. If one of your guys gets hit by a pitch, the next time the opposing team is up to bat they can be sure there's going to be a pitch thrown at a batter. So the Spaniards yelled at us and we yelled back at them. It erupted into this big thing.

Alcalá, who ended up winning overall, was one of the bigger riders in the peloton, and he took the Spanish side in this dispute. Lance was young, 21 then, a kid and a first-year pro.

The young Texan wasn't cowed.

"Shut the hell up!" Lance bellowed "Calm down!"

A lot of the Spaniards didn't speak English, but they knew what he meant. The whole thing calmed down. I won the sprint and ended up winning the King of the Mountains jersey. Alcalá rode for WordPerfect at the time, but he and Lance later became teammates on Motorola.

The next year of the Tour DuPont was an entirely different story. I had high hopes for a result on the GC, or the overall classification. My goal was to place in the Top 10 overall. But the race would become a brutal confrontation with the dope-infused riders of the European peloton. My friend Scott Fortner and I were in the bathroom before the race and saw two guys in one stall. We spotted their bike shoes in the gap below the stall door.

We heard one guy say, "Poco más" — a little more.

Then we heard a clang and saw a syringe drop to the bathroom floor. Scott and I glanced at each other and got the hell out of there.

I thought: *Oh lord. This is going to be a long day.*

I wasn't wrong. That day was one of the most miserable days of my life on the bike. The route was about 135 miles long with a brutal climb near the finish. About 90 miles into the race a big breakaway formed of some twenty riders. It was the break of the race — Lance Armstrong, Greg LeMond, Steve Bauer, Viatcheslav Ekimov — all the main contenders were there, and me. We all worked together and got a significant gap on the peloton.

As we hit the climb, the group started to thin and riders fell off the pace. The climb steepened and Lance attacked hard. The group shattered, but I went with Lance. Then it was down to maybe four guys. LeMond had been popped. Bauer had been popped. I was hanging on for dear life on Lance's wheel. I dug deep. I wanted to make it but I went so deep into the red zone that I blew like I had never blown before.

It was a complete detonation. It's like I went from 110 percent to barely being able to get up the hill. I had to do the "paper boy route," swerving back and forth just to get up the mountain. I went way, way too deep. Once I made it to the top I couldn't descend very well either because I didn't have the strength to control my bike. The final miles into town were rolling terrain — typically where I could use my power. I was probably riding 15 miles an hour slower than everyone else. I may as well have been on a beach cruiser. I could barely turn the pedals over.

In the last twenty miles of the race I lost 20-30 minutes. I was shattered physically and emotionally. It took several months before I felt fit again. That's what happens when you compete clean with dopers. The chemicals in their bodies allow them to go at a harder pace for a longer period of time. I was good enough to get in the break, to be in position, to be one of the last riders on the climb.

I was stupid, too. I shouldn't have gone that deep, but I wanted to show those bastards that I was just as tough and strong as they were. I wanted to get a good result. When Lance attacked it was like nothing I had ever seen before; the power was unbelievable. He had a vicious acceleration on those climbs.

What does it feel like to blow? Imagine you are running a marathon and suddenly the pace picks up to around 4-minute miles and you are now sprinting and you hold that sprint longer than you should but you still have eight miles to go with no gas left in the tank. You blow. Now you are going to be walking the last eight miles. There was nothing in my arms or legs. They were numb. I'm surprised I even finished the race.

My LA dad came out to watch me that day. He would always come out to the Tour DuPont and watch three or four stages and take me to dinner.

He told me later: "I had never seen you like that. You were always a positive person. I had never seen you more physically or mentally shattered than you were that day."

He was sitting at the finish line in the VIP area and the race was on television, so he saw me blow and then he saw me come in literally 20 minutes after everybody else finished. I don't really remember the specifics, but apparently at dinner that night I couldn't even talk — couldn't form words. I was completely drained.

I finished both the day and the stage race, but I was a shell of my former self for weeks afterward.

A marquis professional race for me was the 1994 Road World Championships in Sicily. That race was really a gauge of my talent and is one of the results I am most proud of. I finished seventeenth in the time trial, which was a 42-kilometer race against the clock in Catania, on the east coast of Sicily. I raced to my full natural potential. My average heart rate for that race was 191— for nearly an hour. I could not have gone any harder. My max heart rate was 202, and I hit my max during the race. That's the level of fitness I had. It put me about 3 minutes and 20 seconds away from being World Champion. Future Tour winner Jan Ulrich was third, just 1 minute 52 seconds ahead. A mere 3.5 percent increase in my performance and I would have been the World Champion — clean.

I know what some other riders were taking. Steroids, from my understanding now, would have given me at least 1.5 to 2.5 percent improvement. 2.5 percent gets me in the Top 5. Almost everybody did steroids. Most people even today refer to roids as "low octane." The drug gives you better recovery so you can train harder, which means you're fitter and faster. EPO with my low natural hematocrit would have led to a significant increase. Had I done the full cocktail of drugs, I could have conservatively expected at least a 5–8 percent improvement in my performance.

EPO alone is expected to give an endurance athlete an improvement of up to 10–15 percent, especially for somebody with a low hematocrit — 40 — like mine. When I look now at the list of riders who finished ahead of me, I see a lot of guys who are known and self-confessed dopers and others who are suspected of being dopers. I did not understand then the full extent of doping. I heard the rumors and maybe I was naïve, but my goal was to crack the Top 10. I was just 40 seconds away from realizing that goal. How many in the Top 10 honestly did it clean? I would like to know.

With fractions of seconds between winners and losers, equipment is also a factor. I made a bad decision about my helmet in Sicily. It was really hot at the start, and a guy was trying to be helpful, but in retrospect I wish he wouldn't have said anything. It was one of the American officials.

"You're a pro. You don't have to wear a helmet," he said.

I was a minute from my start and the Sicilian heat was searing, plus the pros were too cool to wear a helmet, I was led to believe, and I wanted to look cool, too.

However, the aerodynamics of a helmet make you faster — significantly faster. The aerodynamic advantage of a helmet alone is estimated to be over 60 seconds on a 40-kilometer course. Of course it was more comfortable without the helmet, so who knows. Maybe I would have overheated with it on.

You can't rewrite history. I have to be objective. Seventeenth to me doesn't sound great, but when you are talking about seventeenth best in the world, that is pretty big. When you are a World Champion, that translates to a minimum seven-figure contract. Plus, there never has been an American Men's World Champion in the time trial. Lance Armstrong and Greg LeMond have won road World Champions, and Tyler Hamilton won a gold medal in the Olympics, although he was stripped of his title after getting caught blood doping. But no American male has won the time trial at the World Championships. A time trial is called the race of truth because there are no tactics, no team working for you. The variables are pretty much the same for everybody. It is you against the clock.

I had an uncanny ability to punish myself, especially in a time trial. The effort was so painful it was sick. You almost had to welcome the pain because otherwise you were going to fail. You had to be fast; you had to go right to the edge. Go too hard, though, and you blow. I wore my heart-rate monitor, but I strapped it face down so I wouldn't look at it. I thought, *I'm just going to race my race by feel.* If I had looked at my heart-rate monitor I probably would have freaked out and backed off. I was on the verge of blowing the whole way, which is exactly where you have to be in a time trial — on the verge of going too far into the red.

At the finish line, I knew I had given my best. There was no way I could have gone any faster, clean. I had given up the second half of my season to train for one race. I had trained with Coach Carmichael and the national team in Winter Park — specific time-trial training. I'm thankful my team let me miss all those races to train for the World's. I was disappointed then, but knowing what I know

now, seventeenth was a respectable result. This was only my second season as a pro and fourth season ever, and I was representing the U.S. at the World Championships.

And besides, I had other races in which I could prove myself.

Photo credit: Linda Mercier

I raced in the four-man team time trial at the Barcelona '92
Summer Olympics. I'm third from the left at the starting line.

From 1993–1996 I was a member of the Saturn Cycling Team,
where I increased my bike-handling skills and set my sights on
competing in Europe.

Photo credit: Mandie Mercier
I'm hoisting the victory bouquet at the 1996 Giro del Capo (Tour of the Cape), a five-stage race around Cape Town, South Africa. Saturn Cycling Team also competed that same trip in the Tour of South Africa, called the Rapport Tour.

Photo credit:
Paula Marzella

I met my future
wife, Mandie,
after winning
the 1996 Tour
of South Africa,
which was my
biggest win on
Saturn. Mandie
is a native of
South Africa
and an avid
cyclist.

This is my family in Telluride: Mom Susan, Telluride Dad Bill,
brother Blake, and sister Lorraine.

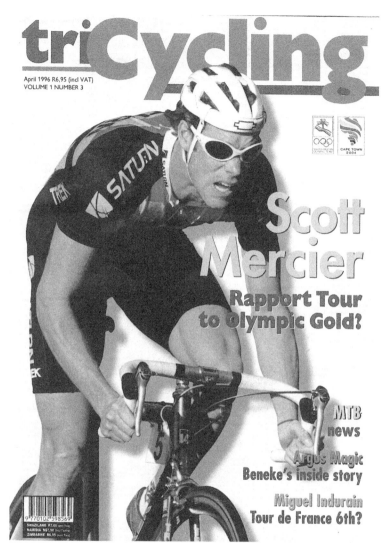

My Rapport Tour win garnered the cover of triCycling magazine in April 1996. As to the Olympic speculation on the cover, I did try out for the 1996 Olympics, but a broken chain and bike change in the first race ended my hopes as I got dropped from the winning break.

dob:	24 January, 1968
age:	29
nationality:	American
residence:	Boulder, CO
height:	6'3"
weight:	175 lbs.
pro since:	1991

This is my 1997 U.S. Postal Service Professional Cycling Team athlete's card. At 6'3" I was a pretty big for a climber. My race weight was 168 pounds.

Traditionally one of America's finest time trialists and climbers since he came onto the cycling scene in 1991, Mercier began his 1996 season with a successful trip to South Africa, winning a pair of stage races - the Rapport Tour and the Giro del Capo. In the U.S., the 1993 Tour DuPont King of the Mountains won the Tour de 'Toona. In 1995, Mercier finished second overall at Australia's Herald Sun Tour and fourth overall at the Tour of China.

Top Results

1996	
1st	overall, Rapport Tour
1st	overall, Giro del Capo
1st	two stages, Tour de 'Toona
1st	overall, Tour de 'Toona
2nd	stage, Rapport Tour
2nd	two stages, Giro del Capo
3rd	two stages, Rapport Tour
3rd	stage, Giro del Capo
3rd	two stages, Herald Sun Tour
5th	stage, Giro del Capo
9th	overall, Herald Sun Tour
1995	
1st	Unaweep Canyon Road Race
1st	stage, Herald Sun Tour
1st	stage, Sarasota Stage Race
2nd	overall, Herald Sun Tour
2nd	time trial, National Championships
3rd	overall, Tour de Toona
4th	overall, Tour of China
8th	overall, Redlands Classic
1994	
3rd	overall, Australia Alpine Tour
1993	
1st	mountains classification, Tour DuPont
1992	
Olympic Team Member	
1st	TTT, National Championships

Scott MERCIER

The back of my 1997 U.S. Postal Service Professional Cycling Team athlete's card lists my racing results.

Photo credit: Mandie Mercier
In 1997 I suffered a devastating crash at the Boland Bank Tour, my final race as a professional. I endured two surgeries over eight hours to reconstruct my face.

Photo credit: Joel Cantor
George Hincapie and I participated in the 2013 Denver Post Ride the Rockies prologue fundraising event in Telluride, Colorado. We had been teammates during the 1992 Olympics and roomed together in Girona, Spain, while on the U.S. Postal Service Team in 1997.

I took this photo with my daughter, Mira, on a family vacation to
Croatia in August of 2019.

Chapter 9

WIN AS A TEAM

Cycling, like life, is a team sport.
Everyone plays their role for the team's success.

No matter your role, there is strength in being the humble servant. One cyclist may cross the finish line first, but the rest of the team helped get him there. Sometimes you work for others, and sometimes they work for you. You bring your best individual effort to strengthen the team as a whole.

Saturn was invited to the national Tour of South Africa, called the Rapport Tour, in 1996. This time was a historic turning point in South Africa's struggle for racial equality. Nelson Mandela had been elected the country's first president following the dismantling of the racial segregation of apartheid, and we were one of the first professional sports teams from the United States to compete in the country, following years of international boycotts.

I was excited to visit Africa, and South Africa in particular. The Rapport Tour was an eleven-day, 1,440- kilometer stage race from Johannesburg to Cape Town. Steve Bauer, Norm Alvis, Bart Bowen, Mike McCarthy, and I were selected to represent our team. The staff consisted of race manager Rene Wenzel, mechanic Vincent Gee, and soigneur Paula Marzella. It was going to be a four-week trip and include both the Rapport Tour and the Giro del Capo (Tour of the

Cape), a five-stage race around Cape Town.

We arrived a week before the Rapport Tour. I bought a Lonely Planet travel guide because I thought: *Shoot, when am I ever going to be back in Africa? I've got to check some things out.* The trip became more than a race; it became an expedition. Mike McCarthy would tell me years later that the experience of the Rapport Tour was one of his fondest cycling memories.

Americans were an anomaly in South Africa then, and wherever we went we were the object of good-natured curiosity. The Cricket World Cup was on, and friendly South Africans tried to teach us the complicated rules of cricket. After raucous pub primers on stumps, bails, and wickets, we let the Lonely Planet travel guide lead us around the Rainbow Nation.

We toured the town of Oudtshoorn, which in the 1930s and 1940s was the ostrich capital of the world. Ranchers domesticated ostriches and raised them for their plumes for fashionable hats, for their lean meat, and later for their skins as exotic leather.

I'd read in the guide that Pilansburg, a small national park home to the Big 5 of Africa, was a few hours' drive away from our hotel in Johannesburg. Everyone was game for a Big 5-spotting safari. The whole team piled into two small rental cars and drove to the park in search of big game. February is late summer in South Africa, and the savannah grass swayed high. Our econo rental cars slung low to the ground, and we struggled to see over the tall grass. I had the idea we could sit on top of the cars with our legs jutting out the window openings. Bart Bowen was our chief spotter, seated on the roof of the car. With arms and legs akimbo, we looked like oversized tourist clowns stuffed into undersized Shriner cars.

We followed every rutted, dirt road. Our quest was to locate as many of the Big 5 as we could find and check them off the list.

We spotted a giraffe and were psyched because the giraffe had to be one of the Big 5. It's the tallest animal in Africa, towering over 18 feet tall. Our next Big 5 sighting was of some immense, porcine hippos. Then we came across a rocky outcropping, probably 30 feet high, with a sign that read: "Danger, lions. Remain in your vehicle."

Jackpot!

Stupid American tourists that we were, we scrambled out of the cars and climbed the outcropping, scanning the area for lions like it was a freaking zoo. It's not like the lions had read the sign and would be sitting there waiting for us. Lucky for us they weren't, and we didn't see any.

Later on, a game ranger came by in a Land Cruiser and saw these eight idiot Americans tooling around sitting on the roofs of their cars. I was driving, and I had one leg hanging out and the other in the car to push the gas and the brake.

The ranger yelled at us, "You're going to dent the roof of your car!"

We waved away his concern in unison with, "It's a rental!"

Months later, I found out we actually hadn't seen any of the Big 5. The Big 5 are not the five *largest* animals in Africa, but the five *most dangerous* animals to hunt in Africa: the lion, elephant, rhino, Cape buffalo, and leopard.

Better to stick to racing than safariing.

The Rapport Tour began in Johannesburg on February 21. The first stage was windy with medium-sized rolling hills. The wind made for fast racing, and there was tension in the bunch. I attacked on one of the rollers about 20 kilometers from the finish of the stage and quickly was joined by Michael Rich, a German, and the Rapport Tour winner in 1994, local favorite Andrew McClain, and Kazakhstani rider Andrei Kivilev.

We worked well together and quickly built a lead of about 60 seconds. With four strong teams represented, this breakaway had a realistic chance of succeeding. I'd studied the race bible and knew there was a sharp, right-hand corner about 400 meters from the finish line. A race bible is a booklet with descriptions of each stage including distance, start time, estimated finish, elevation gain, and a detailed map of the last kilometer.

My studying paid off, and I strategized how to use that final, sharp turn to my advantage. We flew to the final kilometer as a squadron of four. I knew what to expect and the only way to win.

Sprinting was not my forte, so I knew to win the stage I was going to have to be smart. I attacked our group coming into the final corner and built a lead of 20 meters. But it was just too far to sustain to the finish line. With 40 meters to go, Rich caught me and jumped past. Rich finished first, I finished second, and we had a gap of 1 second on Kivilev and McClain, and 45 seconds on the rest of the peloton.

This time gap earned me the leadership role on our team as the best chance to win for Saturn. That meant team members would work for me and try to position me so I could win the race. The next several stages saw no significant changes in the overall standings. We took some pointed ribbing from local media for our storied touristing, which didn't go over well with our team. Prior to the fourth stage, a local reporter observed to Norm Alvis, "It seems like you Yanks are just here on holiday. " Norm protested that I was second overall, so clearly we were taking the race seriously. It pissed us off, quite frankly, and provided additional motivation to prove to South Africa and the rest of the world that the Americans were here to top the podium.

Later that same day, Mike McCarthy won the fourth stage. It was a flat stage with a rectangular finish through town. Steve Bauer took Mike to the front with about 300 meters to go, and the former World Champion would not be denied. There were three German National teams in the race, and they were colluding; they were all working together. They had essentially fifteen riders working for one guy, their team leader, and we had five guys with no other help.

As the race continued south toward Cape Town, we crossed the Karoo region of South Africa. It is wide-open terrain with little vegetation and rolling hills — a perfect recipe for heat and wind. The fifth or sixth stage delivered some unintended help. The race leader, Michael Rich, flatted. I was still in second place and Norm asked me, as the team leader, "Merce, what do you want to do?" It's not blatantly unethical, but there's a gentleman's agreement to not attack when the race leader flats. I was conflicted. I wanted to win, but I also had been attacked when I flatted while leading and didn't believe it was sporting.

"Let's wait," I said.

Steve, who won an Olympic silver medal, spent eleven days in the yellow jersey of the Tour de France, won Classics, and is regarded as one of the best Canadian cyclists of all time, strongly disagreed. He got the team together at the front of the peloton and rode hard. He said to Norm, "We're riding!"

He then yelled to me: "We are outnumbered and we're riding. You sit on the wheels and don't touch the wind!"

The Karoo wind was a howling cross-tailwind. Steve put the team on the front to start driving the pace. This type of wind is dangerous because the speeds are really high and it is difficult to get a draft as the peloton echelons across the road. The field quickly started to shatter. Within a few kilometers it was down to about fifteen to twenty guys. Steve had four guys driving the pace as hard as they could and most of the rest of the field was in the gutter.

I had the sweet spot. I was sitting fifth wheel and not touching the wind as Steve, Bart, Norm, and Mike buried themselves. They made it easy for me. The four rode a flat-out team time trial, echeloning across the road. No other riders helped, and if you're not going to work— which nobody was — you were in the gutter. Unlike the Ruta Mexico, my first race as a professional, this time I was the gatekeeper, and I didn't let any rider who wasn't going to pull get a draft.

We totally destroyed the race. By the time Michael Rich got a wheel change he was over a minute behind and his race was in jeopardy. It took Michael and the rest of the Germans about an hour, probably 45 to 50 kilometers, to catch back up to the front of the race. They must have been in a panic because they were drafting cars and hanging onto them, against race rules. Hein Verbruggen, who was head of the UCI at the time, came to South Africa to watch the race as a show of support for the globalization of cycling, beyond its Eurocentric roots. Because of the heightened international profile of the Rapport Tour, officials had less tolerance for scofflaws.

Uwe Peschel, one of the Germans hanging onto cars, was kicked out of the race. I think officials kicked out two guys total for hanging onto cars. The Germans lost two of their fifteen teammates, and when they finally caught up to us, Jens Voigt was bright-red with anger. Drenched in sweat, he rode up to Steve yelling, "You are no sportsman!"

Steve shot right back: "Don't talk to me about sportsmanship! You've got fifteen people working against us, colluding!"

When Rich was back in the group we eased up and Steve pulled me aside and said: "Look, Merce. You're too nice. If you want to win this thing, we've got to take any advantage we can. We won't attack them again today on the climb. They're praying to God you don't attack them today. We won't do that, but we had to send them a message and make them earn this thing. I once saw Sean Kelly attack another Irishman in Paris-Nice when he flatted. That's racing."

That was a big lesson for me.

A few days later I took the lead and, once again, Steve taught me another valuable lesson. We missed the breakaway. Four guys got away and we didn't have a rider in the breakaway. The Germans had two of the four guys in the breakaway, and no one in the field was willing to chase them down. This breakaway got 12, 15 minutes up the road, so essentially, we had lost the race — it was over. If we didn't start chasing, there was no way to win.

Steve directed the team: "Get to the front! We're taking control of this race! We're working. Merce can win this race, and if we want to win the race we have a responsibility to take control. We are the only ones who can do it."

Once again, I was in the sweet spot. I wasn't touching the wind. The guys just started doing another team time trial — not as hard this time, but certainly at an uncomfortable pace. That was a 220-kilometer day, the longest and hardest of the race. The bigger climbs were near the end, but the mid-section of the stage was mostly flat, open road with a few rolling hills. The lead of the breakaway slowly started to decline … from 15 minutes … to 12 minutes …10 … 8 … 6. The team just put their heads down and rode. Nobody was helping us — none of the Kazakhstanis, none of the Russians, none of the South Africans — nobody. We had sole responsibility to bring this breakaway back and it was starting to get hilly. When we started to hit the climbs, the lead was down to 3 or 4 minutes and I was feeling good.

"I gotta go. I can catch them. Let me attack," I told Steve.

He grabbed me by my jersey.

"Don't go until I tell you to go. Sit on the wheel. Sit on the wheel!" He wanted it to be crystal clear. "We are going to catch these guys at the base of the last climb and when we catch them, you're on your own. You hit them with everything you have, and you'd better attack as if your life was on the line!"

Sure enough, we caught them at the base of the very last climb, just like Steve said we would. By then, I was terrified. I didn't want to let Steve and the rest of the guys down, so I attacked with an unbelievable rage. I went with everything I had and shattered the field. I got a huge gap and there was no way I was going to let my teammates down. They'd just spent five hours in the wind and the sun and the hills burying themselves to put me in a position to win.

It was one of the most humbling experiences of my life. I'd done a lot of work for other people in my cycling career, so I knew the sacrifice they were making. Sometimes you can push well beyond your abilities for a team leader. And I had one of the best English-speaking cyclists in the world, Steve Bauer, going up against the race manager and working his ass off for me to win.

As I was coming up to the top of the climb, I saw one rider bridging up to me: Jens Voigt. There were time bonuses at the top of the climb and I needed the time. It became a drag race between Voigt and me, but he was slowly closing the gap. Something clicked in my brain and I remembered what Alexi Grewal had taught me about breakaways. Alexi was the 1984 Olympic road race gold medalist. He and Steve had been in a breakaway at the Olympic road race in Los Angeles and Alexi managed to outsmart Steve and beat him.

Alexi is a Colorado guy. He grew up in Aspen and lived in

Boulder, where I occasionally joined him on training rides. We were never teammates, but the seasoned veteran generously offered the up-and-comer tips. With Jens closing in on me, I remembered what Alexi told me about breakaways: If you're up the road and somebody is bridging up, you gotta let them catch you. The finish line for them is your wheel, so they can go harder than you can because they have a shorter distance to go. So when you see that guy, don't turn it into a time trial. Back off to 75, 80 percent, but not so much that it looks like you sat up. And when he catches you, attack him immediately because he's going to be on his limit, while you've had a slight recovery.

My rear wheel, I realized, was the finish line for Jens and he was going to catch me, so I eased up a bit. When he got to my rear wheel I immediately counter-attacked him and made it to the top of the climb to get the time bonus. The finish line was still about 15 kilometers away from the top of the climb, and a group of four riders including Jens, Alexander "Vino" Vinokourov, and Sergei Ivanov caught me as we raced toward the line. I didn't care how I finished on the stage, so I kept driving the pace. Vino and Ivanov occasionally lent a hand, but it was mostly just me racing as hard as I could.

Jens was sitting on and won the sprint. I think Vino was second, and I got third, but we put about a minute into the race leader Michael Rich, who was my main rival for the overall. I had taken the lead. I was so dehydrated at the end of the stage that the race doctor gave me two liters of saline solution in IV bags — now IVs are banned but they were allowed back then — and still I didn't pee all night. It was a hard day. The temperatures hovered between 95 to 100 degrees for six-plus hours in the saddle, and the team had been in the front controlling the race for me all day.

I kept the race lead the rest of the way, but Rich kept chipping away. He took some significant time out of me in the time trial, but I kept the jersey. No one on the team was climbing well, and I was frequently isolated on the climbs with no teammates to assist me. It would just be me with a handful of Germans, some Kazakhs, Russians, and a few South Africans. But, sure enough, the team would come back up to the group after the climbs. They wouldn't quit and they'd go to the front and keep me sheltered.

The Germans may have kept isolating me, but they couldn't get rid of me. The day I knew I was going to win the race was after one of the intermediate time bonus sprints. The sprint was after a long climb, and once again I was on my own. There were probably eight to ten riders in this group, including three or four Germans, and Rich. He was a decent sprinter and we were separated by only about 10 seconds for the overall lead. It was one of those rare moments where everything aligned, and I could see things happen before they actually did. I knew the Germans would lead Rich out for the sprint and that one of his teammates would try to create a gap between us.

The Russians and the Kazakhs were actually pretty gracious in these sprints. They were not trying to mess with our fight for the overall win. Rich had two teammates keeping the speed high as we got close to the sprint line, and Voigt was on his wheel. That left me in fifth position. I knew Voigt was going to try to gap me off. He had Rich right in front of him and I just knew he was going to open up a gap to try to take me out of the sprint. It was at about 500 meters to go when Voigt started to drift off Rich's wheel to open the gap.

We were flying at probably 35 miles an hour. As soon as I saw the gap open to a wheel length, I went by Voigt and knocked him out of the way. Now I was on Rich's wheel, exactly where I needed to be. His last guy pulled off and the sprint started at about 200 meters to go. I went with all I had and waxed him to win the sprint. Instead of losing time in the sprint, I actually took a second out of him. They could do everything they wanted — they had four teammates. Voigt was trying to gap me off, but I was not going to lose.

I've got to hand it to Rich and the rest of the Germans. They fought all the way to Cape Town and kept attacking the entire way. On the last climb, Rich kept attacking and attacking, but I was able to cover his moves and with 10 kilometers to go, he sat up and shook my hand. The race finished below Table Mountain on the waterfront of Cape Town. It was a beautiful setting and a massive relief. After twelve days of racing and nearly 1,500 kilometers, I had won. And I won by just 9 seconds.

In any stage race, there is a lot of down time. Sometimes on the longer days the race will go along at a leisurely pace — almost like a touring pace. As Americans in South Africa, we were an anomaly, and we befriended many of the South African competitors. I clearly remember South African rider Jacques Louis Van Wyk telling me in his heavy Afrikaner accent: "Wait till we get to Cape Town, man. Beautiful Afrikaner women in Cape Town!"

Prior to the final stage in Cape Town, Steve had told me to pack a bag because we were going out to celebrate what was sure to be my first big win. I was wary that the celebration could be premature.

"I only have a 9-second lead," I cautioned. I had reason to be worried. During the 1995 Sun Tour, the biggest race in Australia, I'd lost on the last day after having led the entire race. It was horrible. I was in tears.

"Don't worry about it. You're gonna win this thing," Steve assured me.

He was right. Riding into Cape Town was one of the more rewarding days of my professional life.

After the podium celebration, Steve and I had dinner and a few drinks by ourselves and then joined the team and the rest of the racers at the post-race party. I was in a good mood, had good reason to celebrate, and had consumed way too many drinks. The party was filled with bike racers, but there were very few women in sight. It looked like a pickle salad. I complained to Jacques Louis: "What the hell? Where are all the beautiful Afrikaner women you promised?"

He smiled. "I know one!" The next thing I knew a beautiful petite blonde with a welcoming smile was standing in front of me.

"What are you drinking?" I asked her.

She answered, "Castle Lager," which is the South African equivalent of a Budweiser.

"Good. Get two," I replied.

This beautiful woman walked away without saying a word,

retrieved two beers, pressed one in my hand and then disappeared. I'm sure she was thinking, *What an asshole.*

After that, I chased her for quite some time throughout the night and finally learned her name — Mandie — and convinced her to dance with me.

As she was leaving I asked for her phone number. The next day I called and some guy answered the phone. It was my biggest South African rival, Andrew McClain.

Apparently Mandie hadn't wanted to give me her real phone number, so she gave me the first number that came to mind. She probably didn't think I'd call anyway. Andrew raced for Mandie's dad's team. My call to Andrew's phone interrupted a team meeting. The entire team was discussing tactics for the upcoming stage race, The Giro del Capo, and how they could beat me and the rest of the Saturn team.

Mandie said the room went completely silent when Andrew answered his phone, turned to her, and said: "It's Scott Mercier. He wants to talk to you."

Our first date was at a nice restaurant on the waterfront. We took a sunset ferry around the harbor. I worked up the courage to hold her in my arms. I will never forget that night. We spent hours talking and getting to know each other, falling in love.

Racing, though, was still my first love.

The Giro del Capo was a five-day stage race around Cape Town. Andrew won the opening time trial for Mandie's dad's team, Deo Gloria, and I placed second for Saturn. Stage Two was a road race on rolling terrain. Andrew's team consisted of mostly young, inexperienced riders, many of whom had not even finished the Rapport Tour. The stage started fast with lots of attacks. Andrew directed his team to chase them all down. We decided to get in on the attacks as well and Mike McCarthy attacked hard. Mike quickly got a decent gap.

By having his team chase down all early attacks, Andrew's strategy was for Deo Gloria to take control of the race immediately, but his young riders didn't have the legs to see it through. They'd burned all their matches a tenth of the way into the race.

Andrew chased Mike himself. He was able to bring Mike back within a few kilometers but I noticed that as the chase went on Andrew's arms started flapping — a tell-tale sign of exhaustion. I was sitting right on Andrew's wheel. By the time he caught Mike, Andrew's arms were flapping like duck wings and I knew he was at his limit.

The stage was short, but there was still around 60 kilometers left to race. When we caught Mike, I decided I would attack. I instantly got a good gap and looked back to see what was happening in the race. A lone Russian rider was trying to bridge up, so I waited for him to catch me. I figured that two riders had a better chance of making it to the finish and I knew the Russians would not chase their own teammate. They also did not have a rider who had finished within a minute of me in the time trial, so I knew he wasn't a threat for the overall. We put our heads down and rode at a hard, steady tempo and we built a steady gap. We finished with a lead of nearly 2 minutes on the peloton.

The last stage started in predawn darkness at 6 a.m., which was an unusual early-morning start for a professional race. We didn't know it — we were in our own little cocoon as professional cyclists — but this day also included the Cape Argus, a fun race and the largest one-day, timed cycling event in the world. All the pros were entered in the stage race for the Giro del Capo, but unbeknownst to us, we also were the kickoff to this huge, amateur cycling event. It was like the New York Marathon, only on bicycles. We didn't realize that this last stage was also its own significant event, and not just part of overall tour standings.

With about 15 kilometers left in the race, Steve and I spotted a German rider up the road, identifiable only by his team kit. I didn't know who he was or if he was in contention for the overall. He was several minutes up the road and we could barely see him on the climb.

"What's going on with that guy?" I asked Steve.

"I'll find out," and Steve rode back to the race manager's car.

"He's no threat," Rene assured. "He's out of contention."

While Steve was in the back of the field, having gone to the team car, I decided to attack. My impatience with this ill-timed attack caused Steve to get blown out the back.

As we were coming into the finish, on the last descent with about three miles to go, a Volkswagen bug veered onto the course. I was in the lead and in the apex of a hard-banked corner, probably going 40 mph, racing full speed. Somehow I was able to break my line, whip back and forth, and not crash. It was the luckiest thing in the world. By that point I knew I was going to win the overall, and I crossed the line in third place to seal the deal.

It's a little bittersweet, though, because if we'd known this one stage was such a singular event, we would have tried to win it.

On our last night in South Africa, Mandie and I went out for drinks and dancing. However, it turned out Mandie was dating a guy named Hannes. He was the only one of us with a rental car, so Steve, Mandie, Hannes, and I all went out together in his car. Every single time we went somewhere, Steve jumped in the passenger seat first. Mandie and I were left to sit together in the backseat. We went from bar to bar, from club to club, and she always had to get in the back. Steve wasn't being an asshole because he wanted to be in the front seat. He specifically sat in the front to force Mandie to sit in the back with me. He never said anything, but I know that was why. This poor guy, Hannes. After Steve and I started getting hammered, we began calling him "Heinous." Then we dropped the H and called him "Anus" all night long.

"Anus, you want another drink?"

"Anus, we're ready to leave."

"Anus, thanks for the ride!"

The guy had the worst weekend ever because he had this jackass American calling him Anus, this Canadian monopolizing the front seat, and his girlfriend relegated to the backseat with the jackass. To top it off, he flew home the next morning to Johannesburg and found out his classic convertible Mercedes had been stolen. I don't know if I'm real proud of my behavior that weekend, but I'm still married to that petite blond Afrikaner.

So that was Steve Bauer — an awesome dude. Not only would I not have won the Rapport Tour if not for him, I wouldn't be married to my wife, either. I think things happen for a reason. I met my wife for a reason, and we met because of her brother. He was nineteen and into cycling, and this was two years before Mandie and I met in South Africa. His name was Marius, which now is our son's name.

August 8, 1994, Marius had gone on a solo training ride in Pretoria. He wasn't wearing a hard-shell helmet. He was wearing one of those helmets called a hairnet, which is leather and foam. As he was leaving the city he was struck by a truck. He wasn't going fast and the truck wasn't going fast, but Marius fell and hit his head on the sidewalk curb. His brain started swelling.

Marius was rushed by ambulance to a private neurosurgical hospital, but he didn't have ID on him and lost consciousness in the ambulance. The hospital would not admit him because they weren't sure he could pay the bill. He lay in the ER for eight hours until he could be transported to a government hospital, where he waited another five hours until a physician was available to relieve the pressure on his brain. By that time it was too late and he was brain dead. It was devastating to the family, to have lost their son and brother so senselessly. The initial hospital was so motivated by profit they let a young man die. So much for the Hippocratic oath.

To deal with his grief, Mandie's dad, Sticks, sponsored a team of his son's friends called Deo Gloria (Glory to God). Sticks had a timber transporting business with hundreds of employees. His company harvested timber for paper mills and mines. Deo Gloria Cycling became one of the top teams in South Africa, with mostly young, aspiring riders. The veteran Andrew McClain was hired to get results and mentor the young riders. Mandie worked human resources for her dad and helped out with logistics for the team.

Mandie and I are together because of cycling. It has caused us both so much pain, but it also brings us so much joy, and it still brings us together today. We take date rides together where we can get away from work, kids, and the stress of daily life. It's become our therapy and has helped strengthen our bond.

Win True

Chapter 10

IF YOU'RE A CHEATER YOU'RE A LIAR

You will always know that your success wasn't earned on a level playing field.

My LA dad has always romanticized the year I lived and trained in Girona, Spain, as a member of the U.S. Postal Service Professional Cycling Team. He calls it Camelot, comparing it to a version of JFK's White House and, in a way, I suppose he's right. Back then we were young, powerful, and on the cusp of greatness. Everything was ahead of us.

"Us" was me, Darren Baker, Tyler Hamilton, and George Hincapie.

In 1997 we lived together in what is now the center of the English-speaking cycling world in Europe. Greg LeMond had lived in Belgium, and 7-11 was the first big professional American team to compete in Europe, but the Postal team was the vanguard of the American invasion of the peloton. It wasn't just an invasion; it was an occupation. We came — and we conquered. The team and its alumni of riders went on to win every Grand Tour, multiple Olympic medals, and dozens of Classics. Postal was by far the most dominant team of the peloton and was arguably one of the most dominant teams in the history of sport.

Nearly every outstanding American cyclist of that generation passed through the doors of Postal or its successor teams of Discovery and Radio Shack: Kevin Livingston, George Hincapie, Tyler Hamilton, Jonathan Vaughters, Floyd Landis, Tom Danielson, Christian Van de Velde, Levi Leipheimer and, of course, Lance Armstrong. There's an asterisk to their historical record, though. Every one of those riders has been implicated or associated with heavy performance drug use.

My move from Saturn to Postal was a combination of being in the right place at the right time and having something that the Postal team wanted: Union Cycliste International (UCI) points.

It also involved being in a wedding party. One of my best friends from college, Brett Weisel, asked me to be a groomsman in his wedding. During the rehearsal dinner in San Francisco, I found myself talking with Brett's dad about cycling. It was more than idle chatter: Brett's dad is Thom Weisel, a successful investment banker, art collector, athlete, and financial backer of Tailwind Sports, which managed Postal.

I'd just come off a great year at Saturn, placing in international races, and Postal wanted to compete on the world tour.

"How many points do you have?" Thom asked of my UCI standing.

I was somewhere around the fourth- or fifth-highest ranked American in the world at that time. I listed my points. "I want to race in Europe next," I said.

"I'd hire you," Thom said. And he did. Among the terms in my new contract was a doping clause. If I got caught doping, I'd be fired. I shrugged it off. *How would that ever affect me?*

Girona is about 20 kilometers from Costa Brava, on the Mediterranean, about halfway between Barcelona and the French border. Girona is in the Catalonia region, and most of the residents were very nationalistic and didn't think of themselves as Spanish, but rather as Catalonians. They even have a separate language, which really confused us.

Luckily, most of the Catalonians also spoke Spanish. Not that this helped me much, but George spoke Spanish. The rest of us were lazy about trying to speak for ourselves, actually, because George's native language is Spanish, and he could always translate for us. One thing was distinctly Spanish about Girona: There was always bullfighting on TV — hours and hours of bloody bullfighting. This was also in the days before ubiquitous cellphones, and it wasn't easy to keep in contact with family.

That tiny little apartment in Girona became the base for American cycling ex-pats. I literally slept in a closet because I was the last one to get there and claim a room. Tyler said everyone drew straws before I got there — and I got the shortest straw — but I don't buy that. And I'm the tallest of those a-holes, too. Well, I guess when George had his bouffant hairdo he was technically taller, but if height is measured to the top of the skull, then I was the tallest. My feet hung over the end of the bed in my closet room.

The key to that place looked like it belonged to a castle. It was about six inches long and a half-inch thick. It was the craziest key I'd ever seen. Despite the exotic surroundings, our place was still a typical bachelor pad. George drove us all nuts because he wasn't the neatest guy. The kitchen sink always seemed to be filled with his dishes and the bathroom sink with his facial hair. Years later, when he and I had dinner during the Tour of California, he told me that when he returned in early 1998, after we had all left, the place was literally crawling with maggots because no one had bothered to take out the trash. He was angry, thinking we'd done it on purpose, but in reality, it was an oversight. In a way, it was a bit of karma for him, to come home to a maggot-infested apartment. The two "clean" guys had left and now just the "dirty" ones remained.

But outside of our cramped apartment, the landscape beckoned. The riding around Girona was spectacular. There were miles and miles of paved roads, with little traffic. Within minutes of leaving town we'd be on country roads winding by cork farms, vineyards, and ancient olive groves, or we'd ride along escarpments high above the Mediterranean Sea.

Neither Tyler nor I was selected to race Paris-Nice, the Race to the Sun, in March, and without a prescribed race-training program, the two of us were free to log five to seven hours a day riding on our own around the region. A regular stop was a small café in Lloret de Mar, a beautiful village along the Mediterranean, where we soaked in the beauty of our surroundings and reflected on how fortunate we were to get paid to ride bikes. Steaming coffee and fresh pastries were part of the ritual.

Girona itself has some spectacular Roman ruins from the ninth century. I loved exploring the town and the region, both by bike and on foot. Our team road director, Johnny Weltz, rented me his old white Renault, and Mandie, now my fiancée, and I explored even farther when she'd visit. We once packed a picnic and drove into the verdant mountains of France and then back to the Mediterranean Sea.

George, Tyler, Darren, and I spent countless hours riding the hilly roads of Girona. The accommodations were cramped and at times it got lonely — and boredom occasionally set in — but overall it was an exciting time in our lives. We were invaders, and we were soon to capture the European peloton. Turns out, though, some of the most successful invaders got an advantage from modern medicine. I wouldn't go so far as to say an unfair advantage, since pretty much everyone was doping, but an advantage, nonetheless. As pervasive as it came to be, though, no one was openly talking about it.

While I raced professionally for five years, I was never really an "insider." There were subgroups and cliques within our Postal team. I suspected then, and I know now, that we were divided into two unofficial but silently understood camps: cyclists who were doping and those of us who weren't.

One spring day George and I went out for coffee. He'd been racing in Europe for three years by then, so I was pretty sure he knew the medical expectations. I decided to flat-out ask him what was going on with doping. I was tired of all the secrecy, and by then I felt George and I could trust each other. We were pretty good friends. We'd spent a lot of time together on the Olympic team in 1992, and here we were on the same professional team five years later.

"George, what's up? Do you have to use drugs to be competitive?" I asked him point-blank.

He didn't give me an answer, really. He was quiet for some time, then he nodded his head. "You have to make your own decision," he said.

I didn't ask about his decision; it was obvious. I probably should have pressed him more, but it was clear he didn't want to talk about it. It was a secret club. I was in the club in terms of racing in Europe, but I wasn't a doper, so I wasn't part of the inner circle. That was probably why Darren and I ended up rooming together most of the time — we weren't in the doping club, plus we got along well.

There was one night, however, when Darren sure as hell wished he had a different roommate. I woke up, still half-asleep, and confused about where I was and who I was with. In the dark I thought Darren was my fiancée. Mandie had just visited from South Africa. I got out of bed bare-assed naked and pulled back the covers on Darren's twin bed.

I heard Darren yell out, "What the fuck are you doing?!"

I can't even imagine his terror in seeing my junk in his face as I was preparing to climb into bed with him. The next morning, I saw Darren had built a wall of pillows along the side of his bed to keep me out.

Adding to the constant conspiratorial atmosphere, road director Johnny Weltz often stopped by the apartment and spoke with George in hushed Spanish so we couldn't understand what they were talking about. Darren and I were sick of being out of the loop, so when George was out of the apartment one time, we searched his room, looking for drugs. True to form, his bed was unmade, and clothes and shoes were strewn across the floor. It didn't take long, however, to notice a shoebox on the floor of his closet. We shook the box and heard pills rattling in plastic.

We opened the lid and saw several bottles of pills: B-12, Iron, Vitamin C, and a little brown prescription bottle labeled Testosterone. It seemed so inconsequential — a small bottle of pills. In retrospect, I'm not real proud of rifling through George's stuff;

in fact, I'm ashamed. We'd violated his private space.

The scenery of Girona might have been unchangingly idyllic, but the racing was getting uglier and uglier. In 1997 EPO use was raging — it was obvious in the superhuman racing results. A test for the drug hadn't been developed yet. I wasn't going to do the drugs, the steroids, the EPO, but clearly others were. As a weak attempt to curb doping, the UCI set a hematocrit threshold level of 50 percent. If a rider's hematocrit level was above 50 percent it was "unhealthy" to race and he had to take two weeks off until it dropped back below the threshold. Hard training was only part of being a professional cyclist competing in Europe. Drug testing was another part of this new equation. My first race with Postal was Milan San Remo: one of the Monuments of cycling. The morning of the race, I awoke to a loud knock on my Milan hotel room door at 6 a.m. and the sound of someone shouting, "Doping control."

I've always been an early riser, but this was an unusual wakeup call. Races in Europe don't start early — usually midday or afternoon.

I opened the door to see a chaperone waiting to take me to a "random" doping control. I was escorted to a hotel room where my blood was drawn and urine collected by medical professionals. Four or five of us had been rounded up for this morning's doping controls.

There were quite a few people standing around during these tests. There were blood techs and doctors, probably half a dozen at least, and officials, usually, and somebody like your team manager — you would always have someone from your team there to make sure protocols were followed, and most likely to help you cheat if you needed to, but that was never an issue for me.

I guess one of the ways you could lower your hematocrit was to drink a lot of water and overhydrate yourself because it thins your blood. If riders had any advance warning about testing they also could receive an IV drip of saline solution, which also thins your blood.

Cyclists got their results instantaneously because these pre-race tests were checking hematocrit levels. Results also were tested in a lab for other PEDs, but the immediate result was a rider's hematocrit. Some of the guys on our team had their own blood spinners so they could know exactly what their hematocrit level was. You'd hear whirring sounds coming from their rooms. In five years as a pro, from 1993 to 1997, I had few random doping tests. We got tested before the Tours of South Africa and Australia. During the Tour DuPont there were random tests after a stage. It was a small sample — a handful of riders from the whole race — so the chances of getting a random test were very slim, at least back then. I was a good result for the team. I probably should have been the token random at every race, so they could say, "Look how clean this sport is."

That day in Milan my blood score came in really low, about 39. I could see the look of surprise on the testers' faces. They'd probably never tested an athlete with blood so thin. They should have warned me that with a score that low I'd have a tough day ahead. It was inevitable I was going to suffer.

Milano, as the race is called, is the first of the great spring Classics. It is 300 kilometers long and starts in the fashion capital of Milan and finishes on the coast of the Mediterranean at San Remo. It is the most important one-day Italian race, and all the top teams were represented with their top riders. What a way to start my European campaign. It would be like starting your first professional football game in the divisional playoffs.

We rolled out of Milan under cool but sunny skies. There was a brisk breeze, but no rain was forecast. The first 20 kilometers were neutral, meaning we rode at a leisurely pace. The flag dropped and the racing began immediately. Within minutes the peloton was single-file. Our speeds were 50-plus kilometers an hour, and we zigged and zagged across the road.

I was in the middle of the field, hanging on for dear life. I could not believe how fast we were going. I looked up and saw guys at the front launching attack after attack in an effort to get into a breakaway. After an hour or so of this a few guys successfully got a gap on the peloton and the speeds reduced to a more manageable pace. But I knew that as we got closer to San Remo, the ferocity of the pace would increase again.

The first and longest climb of the day was the 8-kilometer Passo Turchino. It was 134 kilometers into the race and began in the village of Campo Ligure. Naturally, the feed zone was at the base of the climb. Some idiot thought this would be a great place to attack, so the peloton was full of venom and the speeds were ferocious. I always had problems with low blood sugar and was susceptible to bonking, so I could not afford to miss my feed, especially with nearly 160 kilometers of racing left.

I lunged for my long-handled musette — a cotton bag designed to be handed off to a moving cyclist and slung across one shoulder — filled with three bottles of fluid, panini sandwiches, bars, and gels. Carrying nearly 10 pounds of food and drink, I was quickly spit out the back, but at least I would not bonk due to low blood sugar. I ate and drank as much and as quickly as I could, discarded the musette, and labored up the climb. I got into a rhythm and pedaled at a steady pace. As I crested I wasn't too far behind the peloton and was able to rejoin the group on the descent.

The spectacle of the Mediterranean Sea was breathtaking, but also foreboding. I knew that once we reached the coast and turned west the speeds would increase and that a crosswind from the sea awaited us. Sure enough, once we made the sweeping right-hand turn the tension and pace quickened. There were several small hills along the coast and with each ascent I found myself hanging at the back or getting slightly spit out, but I continued to fight to get back to the peloton.

Our next challenge was the short climb of La Manie. Once again the peloton dropped me. I chased back on, but the yo-yoing was causing me to use a lot of energy and I was burning matches fast. The race was in the gutter and I was suffering badly. The team car pulled up alongside me and Jonny Weltz told me to ease up.

"Pull over at the next feed zone and get into the soigneur's trailing car. Don't kill yourself. You have the Tour of Catalonia in two days," he said.

I couldn't believe it! I had never dropped out of a race in my life, and on my first race with the team the director was telling me to call it a day.

Reluctantly, I eased up and soft-pedaled the next few kilometers to the next feed zone. A half-dozen riders from other teams had been given the same orders. One-hundred-and-forty miles ridden and nothing to show for it. My first Monument and my name would not get listed in the results. It would be the first of many DNFs. I noticed that in some of the regional races the speeds of the peloton would be slightly slower. My assumption is that while most of the riders were doping, it wasn't full-gas as it was in some of the World Tour races such as Milan San Remo, Liege Bastogne Liege, and the Vuelta España. In races like those I could barely hold the wheel, but in most of the regional races I was more competitive and contributed to the success of the team. There still would be a handful of guys absolutely flying, but in general the peloton would be a gear slower in these races.

The Tour of Denmark was a perfect example of this. It was my first race back in Europe after six weeks in the States. We had a Dane, Peter Meinert, who was our designated leader for the GC — the general classification, which is the overall placings in a stage race. Things started well for me in the individual time trial. I placed in the top third of the race. Near the end of the race, Peter had moved into second place on the GC when a dangerous move got up the road. I was near the front and saw the race leader, another Dane and 1996 Tour de France winner, Bjarne Riis, and one other rider power away from the peloton. Peter did not make the move and I knew we would be forced to chase for miles. I got to the front and buried myself and was able to singlehandedly bring the breakaway back to the fold and protect Peter's standing.

I was rooming with George at the time, but he had gotten sick and was watching the race from the TV in our hotel room. He told me after the stage: "Man, Merce, that was unbelievable. You single-handedly chased down Bjarne Riis!" It felt good to have done that, and to have it noticed by my teammate. Regardless, I knew there would be fewer and fewer opportunities for victories in the big races. I had topped out as a clean rider.

Following similar experiences, my clean roommate, Darren Baker, was coming to the same conclusion.

"They don't start you out with a full program," Darren explained. "They wait until you hit rock bottom and then they coax you in with the thought of caring for your body."

There were practiced doping-groomers, mid-level European riders on our team, whom Darren and I called the "lecturists." When the opportunity arose, when we were tired and broken, they would lecture us with false concern: "You need to care for your body. You can't let yourself get run down like that."

Neither one of us bought it. But lots of other racers did.

"I'm 100 percent convinced there's a lot of guys in the peloton who would not have been anywhere near able to make it without medicine," Darren said. "There were guys that were completely made by the doctors."

Darren was pretty outspoken about his beliefs at the time. Our team members gave tacit, nodding approval to his concerns, but they quietly continued with their secret "medical program." I was struggling with my own realization that I could not successfully race much longer without going down a slippery slope. I knew in my heart that doping — and by extension cheating — was not who I was. The sport that I had wholly loved since I was a child, pedaling a 10-speed up a steep mountain road and dreaming of Olympic glory, was now taking a sly sideroad, fueled by illegal drugs and situational ethics. I didn't recognize professional cycling anymore, and I didn't recognize myself in it.

European road racing is amongst the most physically demanding sports in the world. But the mental health aspects of the sport are often overlooked. You're thousands of miles from your home, your culture, your language. Many of us struggled, not just to keep our spirits up, but to stay sane. Mental health was not something that was spoken of; you just had to "man up." Postal soigneur Emma

O'Reilly will always hold a special place in my heart for the way she helped keep me grounded, sane, and healthy. Her ribald Irish sense of humor kept me laughing and smiling. It must have been hard for her as well, as a woman in a traditionally male role. She kept at it far longer than I did.

One great last time, Darren and I were left behind in Girona as our roommates competed somewhere in a Classic. We had an unscheduled week to hang out, talk, and go on training rides. We were unabashed goofballs.

"We used to fantasize that our way to get even with all the cheaters in the sport would be that we could have this magical personal tailwind on command at any time that we could just conjure up and ride away from the peloton, like a 25 mile-per-hour tailwind," Darren recalled.

"It was kind of fun, pretty stupid and silly, but you get in a desperation situation where there's really no hope and you can kind of play around with it and try and make some lemonade out of lemons and at least enjoy yourself with a fantasy, if it's not true in reality."

By late spring of 1997 I was frustrated, exhausted, and needed a break. I was getting my ass handed to me in the bigger races. But my hard work, fruitless as it was, had earned me access to the inner circle, and our team doctor, Pedro Celaya, was about to extend an invitation.

"No racing, for sure you test positive."

Those words, uttered by Dr. Pedro Celaya, are seared into my mind as indelible as the asphalt tattoos in my skin. We had just finished the Tour of Romandie in Geneva, and Pedro asked to meet with me in his hotel room. The room was like most of the hotels we stayed in that spring — a small circular table, a bed, a television, and bathroom — in other words, unremarkable.

But what Pedro said in that unremarkable room changed my career and the course of my life. Pedro pinched the skin on my side, just as he had done at our training camp in January and seemed shocked at how thin I had become.

"Take a week off the bike," he said. "And gain a kilo or two."

Next, Pedro went over my summer racing schedule and the training I'd need to do to prepare. He laid out a sheet of paper with dates — like a calendar — and a training program for the next four weeks before my next race. The bulk of the program consisted of some fourteen days of high mileage combined with intensity. The intervals were to be done at the end of each day — after having ridden four hours or so.

"Why aren't the intervals at the beginning of the rides?" I asked, puzzled by that order.

"The racing in Europe is hard at the end of the race," he explained. "I want your body to adapt to the intensity after a few hours of riding."

Dots and stars were drawn on the days of the calendar; each day had two or three dots, and every third day had a star.

Pedro explained the code: Each dot represented a pill and each star an injection. He reached into his briefcase and pulled out a Ziploc baggie filled with glass vials and green pills.

"Do you know how to inject yourself?" he asked perfunctorily.

"I've never given myself a shot," I confessed.

This surprised him. A tutorial was in order.

Pedro grabbed one of the glass vials and showed mc how to snap off the tip and draw the liquid into a syringe and push the plunger forward to make sure there were no air bubbles. He instructed me to clean my skin with an alcohol swab before injecting.

"What is in the pills and vials?" I asked, nervously.

"Steroids," he said.

There was an uncomfortable silence for a few seconds. I think he sensed my concern.

"Are these going to make my balls shrink?" I asked.

That broke the tension. He laughed.

"These are mild steroids, but you will go strong like bull — stronger than ever before!"

He warned: "No racing, for sure you test positive."

This training block ended on a Friday or Saturday and I was to be racing a week later back in the U.S. At the end of a cycle of pills and shots, the drugs are out of your system in five days. You won't test positive, you're technically clean, and you've had this immense workload you've been able to do before the race.

The prototypical steroid-user people many people think of is Arnold Schwarzenegger — this massive, bulky weightlifter type. But if you're an endurance athlete, steroids let you do a heavy workload again and again. They accelerate your recovery. They make you feel like you can get up and do a hard workout again the next day.

You're going to get lean and hard and strong. Invincible. Superhuman.

"Put these in your pocket, and if you get stopped by customs say they are B vitamins," Pedro instructed.

I stuffed them in my pocket, just like he said, and flew to Johannesburg to spend time with Mandie. I was terrified going through customs with that tell-tale crinkly baggie in my pocket. I felt like a drug dealer. I'm often asked, "Why did you take the bag?" The truth is that I wasn't sure what I was going to do. I just wanted to get the hell out of that room with Pedro.

I knew I had a decision to make about what I was willing to do to be competitive. I sat down with Mandie, the Ziploc baggie between us, and asked what she thought. She looked at the drugs and looked at the training schedule.

"You have to make your own decision," she said finally.

She would later say she thought this was "bush-league medicine. No real doctor tells these kids to inject themselves with needles." But at the time she left it up to me.

Pedro, I believe, wasn't acting with malice toward the riders on Postal. He probably thought he was helping us because we were under his medical supervision — a safer alternative than scoring drugs from some back-alley dealer. If you put it into context, it was the late '90s, and a couple dozen young cyclists had killed themselves with back-alley EPO. I think Pedro really felt he was protecting us —in a way I can understand how he can justify what he did.

I had to think long and hard about whether to take those drugs.

I still think about it. I thought about my career, my profession as a cyclist. I'd just finished a disappointing spring racing campaign — continually stuck in the gutter and getting my ass kicked. Quite frankly, I was not having much fun. I felt like a complete loser and here was a chance to take a significant step forward in my performance.

I tried to imagine how it would end up and I started to get scared. I'm no teetotaler. I've done my share of recreational drugs, but this was different. I don't have an addictive personality, but extreme fitness is a powerful and potent elixir. There are times where you get so fit you welcome the pain. It feels good to push your body and even more so to absolutely put the hurt on your competitors.

If I jumped on that merry-go-round, I knew I'd never be able to get off. It seemed like the first stop on the road to doping hell. My next step would be EPO and whatever else Pedro wanted to shove in a needle in my ass. Results, fame, and cash might follow, but I didn't see how it could end well. It was definitely cheating, but almost everyone was doing it. No one was getting an unfair advantage at this point. The cheating didn't bother me as much as the fact that it would turn me into a bald-faced liar, because nobody was telling the truth about being a doper.

Ultimately, that baggie of drugs ended up hidden away in a drawer at my in-laws' home in Barberton, South Africa. I never took them. Instead, I rested for a week, trained as Pedro had instructed, and raced in the U.S. over the summer. The training regimen was long, hard, and intense. The first two or three days I was able to complete the training. But by the fourth day I was unable to get my heart rate high enough for the intensity needed for the intervals. My muscles just had not recovered enough.

By the fifth day I needed to take a rest. In all I was able to complete 90–95 percent of the training program. But that final 5–10 percent is what really makes a difference. I still got fast and strong, but I was missing that "Vitamin B" afterburner of strength and power.

It was clear my professional racing career was at a tipping point, and if I was going to tip to the winning side with the juiced-up European peloton, I would need that baggie, and then another one, and then another one … I took the summer to weigh my options. An upcoming family wedding in August would give me time to think, away from the sport, and to make a final decision.

That became my deadline.

Win True

Chapter 11

MAKE A BOLD MOVE

Plan what you can but keep moving forward.

I made up my mind to end my professional racing career and join my LA dad in the restaurant business while staying at the same hotel Stephen King had holed-up in to write *The Shining*. You know that movie where Jack Nicholson's character goes cabin-fever crazy and tries to murder his family with an axe? Yeah, that one.

Heeeeeere's Johnny!

I should have known that was not a good omen.

Infamous for inspiring King's fictional Overlook Hotel, the 1909 opulent resort is an hour from Denver and six miles from Rocky Mountain National Park, in Estes Park. It also was the site of my sister Lorraine's wedding to Paul Weissman on August 7, 1997.

So in-tune was my family to my racing career that Paul and Lorraine moved their wedding from July to August, just on the off-chance I made the Tour de France team.

For several days our blended families basked in the beauty of the Rocky Mountains, Lorraine and Paul's happiness, and each other's company. But my future with Postal weighed on my mind.

I had some tough decisions to make and, at twenty-nine, I wasn't entirely equipped to make them. Over breakfast one day at the Stanley Hotel, my LA dad started talking about "the family business," meaning restaurants.

"I could use your help in a business I recently bought, a string of restaurants in Hawaii," he offered. He had bought twelve beachfront restaurants out of bankruptcy as a turnaround project.

He'd relocated there, too. I was pretty sure I was going to quit racing, but I had no idea what I was going to do next. Fortunately I had a college degree, so unlike a lot of my team members, I had options. I again considered going back to school to get a master's degree or working in financial management, but nothing was jumping out at me as The Just Right Decision. Being a professional athlete is a hard act to follow and there are no guidebooks or support groups to help former athletes make informed decisions.

I know my dad didn't really need my help. He just wanted to work with his son. I'd always wanted to work with my dad, too. I thought it'd be cool. As a kid I always wanted to be like him. I didn't get to see much of him, and like many sons I idolized him for a while. Dad told me that when I was done with professional cycling — and he didn't want to encourage me to quit — he wanted to work together.

By the time Paul and Lorraine exchanged wedding vows, I'd made up my mind. It was hard for me to tell our managing director, Mark Gorski, that I'd decided not to continue with the team for 1998. Mark was a 1984 Olympic Gold Medalist and he ran the business side of the team. It was a tough phone call to make, but it had to be done, and sooner rather than later.

We talked in late August. It was important to me that I speak directly to Mark to explain what I was planning to do. I felt I owed the team that. Also, I had been selected to ride the Vuelta and didn't think it would be fair to block a spot if he had someone else he wanted to get in there.

We caught up — casual how-have-you-beens — and then I launched in.

"I've decided to leave the sport and move to Hawaii to work in the restaurant business with my dad," I said.

Mark was gracious and described how he felt when he finally

hung up his wheels. That helped ease my guilt of letting my team down. My leaving wasn't entirely a surprise to him.

"I've heard rumors you might be considering a career change and I'm glad you told me directly," he said.

He then dropped what I considered a bit of a bombshell.

"Well, now I have a spot for Frankie."

I hadn't known that Frankie Andreu was trying to join Postal. I suppose it makes sense because we had become the only American team racing in the European peloton.

Frankie apparently was unhappy with French team Cofidis, where he and Lance had been teammates, and was not going to be offered a contract extension. He was one of Lance's favored domestiques, whose role on the team is to ride out front of the team leader and create a slipstream. I read later that Frankie told Gorski at the 1997 Tour de France he wanted "to ride with these guys and no one else," meaning the U.S. Postal Team.

So I quit because I didn't want to dope and Frankie took my place on the team. The irony to me is that George would later tell me how Frankie, as an older veteran, was a mentor of sorts for him and that Frankie was instrumental in George's progression of doping.

I appreciate the stand Frankie later took when he was among the first insiders to blow the whistle on doping within the peloton. It's entirely possible that without his and his wife Betsy's persistence the world would not know about the doping problems in the European peloton, but Frankie certainly can't take the high moral ground.

Doping is doping.

It's funny how things turn out. My retirement from professional cycling opened the door for Frankie to join Postal and to be part of Lance's winning teams. Frankie and Lance would go on to have a very public, bitter, and acrimonious falling-out. I wonder if I would have received the same wrath from Lance had I kept racing. With the clear vision hindsight allows, I now see how everything fell into place, dramatically changing the dynamics of the Postal team from 1997 to 1998.

Darren left, too, and with both of us out there were no more squeaky wheels. Our departures allowed for the soon-to-be massively successful heavy doping system to move in and take hold. The era of Lance Armstrong at Postal began, as did "the most sophisticated, professionalized and successful doping program that sport has ever seen," according to the U.S. Anti-Doping Agency report.

I'm always going to wonder, *Where could I have ended up? What was my real potential?* My roommate and friend, Tyler Hamilton, went on to race multiple times in the Tour de France and win a gold medal in the Olympic Games, though he was stripped of his title after a positive doping test. I never raced in the Tour de France. I'll never know my full athletic potential. That's the real price I paid. On the other hand, winning at all costs has a price, too. That price is your soul, your integrity, and in many cases, the core of who you are as a person.

Tyler would later tell me, "I wouldn't go back for $100 million," meaning living a lie. It consumed him and turned him into something and someone he was not. Rarely can any of us point to a distinct fork in the road and say with such clarity that a single decision has shaped us in such a profound way. Little did I know that the day I turned away from the needle and left the peloton would in many ways define the rest of my life.

At the time, though, I was just excited about my new business venture and happy to be calling my own shots. When I got back to Spain and told my Postal teammates I was leaving to run a business in Hawaii, they were jealous. Rather than suffering in the trenches of Belgium and Northern Europe, I'd be surfing in Hawaii. It sounded pretty good. It sounded too good. I should have asked a few more questions.

But first, I had one more stop before starting to work on my Hawaiian tan — a final race to really cap my career. You know how a "swan song" can refer to that last phenomenal performance before either retirement — or death? I was just thinking *retirement* swan song.

It was almost more permanent than that.

Chapter 12
FALL DOWN, GET UP, REPEAT

The best way to never lose is to never compete, but you'll never put yourself in a position to win, either.

South Africa has become an important part of my life. It bookended my racing career with both my best and worst races. The 1996 Rapport Tour was the pinnacle of my professional cycling success. Eighteen months later, not only did I not finish a South African race — it nearly finished me.

The Boland Bank Tour, a five-day stage race around Cape Town, was the worst race of my career. My future father-in-law, Sticks, put together a team for my final race. Even though I'd left Postal, I wanted to race on Sticks' team as a show of family support. I also had an alternative motive: I'd only won two races that year, and I was motivated to win the overall event. My fitness was good and I wanted to end my career on a high note. The first stage was a criterium, which wasn't my strength, but I managed to get enough time bonuses that I was in the Top 5. In the second stage, though, I made a strategic blunder that cost me a chance to win.

There's this thing cyclists do called sag climbing as a way to conserve energy. I started at the front and then just climbed slightly slower than the leaders as I drifted back. I was trying to be smart, but I was too clever for my own good. I sag climbed from the front and then about twenty or thirty guys slowly went up the road as I kept sagging back through the main field. I didn't think there was any way that group was going to stay away; the group was too big and the climb wasn't long.

Turns out I was too complacent because that group did stay away and my team and I were forced to chase. No one else was helping. My team was mostly kids and they were doing what they could, but we didn't have the firepower to bring the breakaway group back. I should have realized I was essentially racing alone. Every other team was represented in the break, and they were working together, which rarely happens in a group that big. I was really angry at myself for having thrown away the race. We finished a minute-and-a-half down. The race was essentially over for us.

There was no way I was going to miss the break the third day. I was going to be the aggressor and force it. About a third of the way through the race it started to heat up and I started attacking and counter-attacking — hard. When you attack, you're essentially sprinting. There's a lot of force on the bike.

I was probably going 30 miles an hour when, in an instant, the front tire rolled, hit the fork, and locked up the front of the bike, catapulting me over the handlebars.

I face-planted into the pavement then stood up, wobbly, and felt around the inside of mouth with my tongue to make sure I hadn't broken any teeth. Something felt seriously wrong and I touched my face, realizing blood was gushing out of wounds. Glancing down, I saw a pool of blood that had poured out of my face and neck.

Dazed, probably going into shock, I stumbled over to the bike and foggily tried to figure out what had happened. Our Race Director ran up to me with eyes as big as sand dollars.

"Get on the ground!" he screamed. "Lie down!"

I did as I was told. The ambulance arrived, and the paramedics put a brace on my neck and wrapped my head and face with gauze. They slid a stretcher underneath me as a caution against spinal injury, and the stretcher functioned like scissors, pinching my butt cheeks as the paramedics closed it. I screamed out in pain.

Meanwhile, Mandie heard crackling over the two-way radio: "Massive accident ... head injury ... on the way to hospital."

Thinking back, I can't even imagine how frightened she must have been. Her brother had been killed just two years before in a cycling crash. She didn't have specific information, she didn't even know which hospital the ambulance was headed to, but she just knew I was the one who had crashed.

In the ambulance as we raced to the hospital, my arms strapped against my sides, I start pinching my legs to see if I could feel anything. I was starting to panic because my legs were numb. I pinched harder and harder but felt nothing. I was terrified that I would be paralyzed. But I could see my toes moving, which was reassuring. I figured out later they'd given me a couple shots of morphine, which is why I was numb.

I could see out of one eye, but the rest of my face was swaddled in gauze. When we got to the hospital, the doctor unwrapped the blood-soaked gauze. Once he got it all off, the first thing he said was, "Call plastics."

I knew then that I had a pretty severe injury. Typical for South African hospitals, they wouldn't admit me until they were sure I could pay. They wanted a credit card to put down a deposit. I had come directly from the race to the hospital and they wanted to be sure I could pay. It's not like we race with wallets.

It was such a clusterfuck. I waited probably two hours until they could figure out if I could be admitted and scheduled for surgery. Mandie and her mother were calling all the hospitals in Cape Town to find out where I was and whether I was conscious. After the death of Marius in similar circumstances, they had reason for concern. Quite frankly, it was astounding that someone from the race didn't escort me to make sure I got proper care.

Finally admitted to a semi-private room with four beds, I woke up after the first surgery at 2 or 3 in the morning. I didn't remember where I was. I could hear people talking and started to piece together what was going on.

Across my hospital room, a fellow patient was trying to leave. I'd picked up on some of the details of his injuries. A shipping container at the docks had fallen on his foot and chopped off the front part of it. He was trying to leave so he could go get his paycheck, but the nurses wouldn't let him go.

The guy next to me was blaring the TV so loudly I couldn't sleep. Finally, I lost it and shouted, "Would you turn that fucking TV off!"

Seriously, what kind of jerk has his TV on at 3 a.m. with other patients in the room? I was in no mood to be polite.

By the third day, I'd had enough of the hospital bed and decided I wasn't going to pee in a catheter anymore. With Mandie's help I took my drip and its stand on rollers and hobbled to the bathroom just down the hallway. None of the rooms had a bathroom. It probably took me five minutes to get there because I could barely shuffle. I was still in an incredible amount of pain.

Standing in front of the bathroom mirror, it was the first time I'd seen my face since the crash. I looked like Frankenstein. My neck was swollen with a half-grapefruit-sized goiter poking out the side and it looked like someone had taken a meat grinder to my face. Tracks of black stitches stretched purple swollen flesh together. I was unrecognizable. A monster.

Mandie, who was standing outside the bathroom said she heard me yell: "I am so fucked! I am so fucked! Look at this, I'm a freak! I'm going to be a freak for the rest of my life!"

It was so atrocious, this injury, that it took two surgeries for eight hours to rebuild my face. Medical staff told me later that alarms kept going off during surgery. Below a certain heartbeat they think you're going into cardiac arrest.

The surgeon finally told the nurse: "Turn that off. He's a pro cyclist. His heart rate's naturally low." My sleeping heart rate then was 28 beats per minute.

Oddly, there was only a small crack in my helmet — the bulk of the impact had been on my face. I didn't break my collarbone or my shoulder. They say when your collarbone breaks it's because you put out your hands to stop your fall. I'd crashed so quickly I hadn't even had time to get my hands off the handlebars. I didn't break a single bone. I didn't break any teeth. It was all flesh wounds and a massive concussion.

When I landed, my glasses cut all the way around my eye. It looked like someone had taken a shot glass, broken it, and carved around my eye with the jagged edges. My cheek looked like a Doberman Pinscher had pulled the flesh down with its teeth. There was a quarter-sized hole with no flesh left, probably from a rock. I had road rash all along my face and a shard of the shatterproof glass from my glasses jammed in my neck, missing my jugular by a centimeter.

The plastic surgeon wanted to schedule a skin graft for my shoulder, but I was tired of the hospital. *Screw it. I'm okay with a scar.* So I've got a big keloid — an overgrowth of scar tissue — on my right shoulder that took about three months to heal. All things considered, the surgeon did a great job. My mom always told me that I have a face for radio anyway.

The wreck was national news. "The Rapport Tour winner was in a massive accident" was everywhere in newspaper headlines and television reports.

As I walked the streets of Cape Town in between doctor visits, people would gawk, approach me, and ask "Are you that guy who crashed?"

The Boland Bank Tour was the unceremonious final race of my career.

In my personal life, however, I was celebrating a new beginning.

Mandie and I had planned our formal wedding ceremony for a month later, in November. We'd gotten married officially months before, on May 23, because we thought it would be easier for Mandie to get a Green Card. We planned to spend the summer in the states, come back for this last race, then move to Hawaii to start our new careers in the restaurant business. But it turned out to be more difficult after we were married because she'd already had a visitor's visa.

This took some time to sort out. I have no patience for

bureaucracy. A little cash in the pockets smoothed things along and we were able to expedite her visa. When I consider the cumbersome immigration process today, it's unbelievable that we were able to get her a Green Card in just six weeks.

Our formal wedding ceremony was in South Africa along the border of the Kruger National Park. So my brother, Blake, could attend during a college break, we scheduled it over Thanksgiving. Our family watched us exchange vows under a thatched-roof arbor on a wooden pier over the Crocodile River. My face zig-zagged with angry scars, I wore more makeup than the bride.

I'd chosen honeymooning in Zimbabwe because it sounded exotic and I'd wanted to raft the rapids of the Zambezi River just below the spectacular Victoria Falls. However, with the bacteria in the water and my open flesh wounds, we decided rafting wasn't a good idea. A canoe ride in the calm waters above the falls was a necessary concession.

We shared a canoe and paddled in unison downriver with a guide and a cooler of cold beer, unaware of the danger of hippos lurking below the surface. Several tourists have been killed by these territorial creatures along this very section of river.

The falls are called "the smoke that thunders" by local tribes. You can hear the falls and see the mist from miles away. As you approach, the sound becomes a deafening roar. The surrounding area is like a tropical rain forest, due to the moisture from the constant mist.

We also visited the Kariba Lake, which is similar in size to Lake Powell in the Southwest of the U.S. To get there, Mandie and I chartered a small plane. Elephants lumbered along on the dirt runway, and the pilot had to buzz them to get them to move so we could land. It was a fantastic adventure together.

The race, the crash, the wedding, and the honeymoon behind us, Mandie and I were eager to start our new life together as husband and wife in another paradise: Hawaii.

Chapter 13
KEEP YOUR OPTIONS OPEN

When making a decision seek multiple options.
Get something to say no to.

I may not have been riding a bike for a living anymore, but that didn't mean my wrecking days were over. My business venture in Hawaii was basically a continuation of the Boland Bank Tour crash. My strategy was all wrong, I hit hard, and it left scars — just not the kind you can see.

Mandie and I packed up and flew to Oahu in December of 1997 with a whole lot of expectations — for our marriage, for our careers, and for our future. I didn't know anything about the restaurant business, so I had to learn the hard way. I started as an assistant manager.

My dad had scooped up twelve restaurants out of bankruptcy. First was Sunset Terrace in Waikiki, right above the famous Duke's restaurant. It had great food and fantastic views. But I didn't have much time to gaze at sunsets. Being an assistant manager meant if the cook called in sick, I cooked. If the dishwasher called out, I washed dishes. There were some three dozen entry-level employees in each restaurant to be managed and many toilets to be cleaned.

Six months later I was transferred to a different restaurant, the

Yum Yum Tree, near the Kaneohe Marine Corps base. We served breakfast, lunch, and dinner, but our specialty was breakfast. I thought, *Finally, I'm on my way to being a business partner.* But instead I just learned how to make a mean Eggs Benedict. I thought I would earn equity in my father's business, but that didn't happen. Dad treated me like any other employee — worse, actually, because he didn't want to show any favoritism. I reported to work at 4:30 a.m. and finished my week five days and fifty-five to sixty hours later.

So I slung hash, and Mandie worked as an assistant manager at another Yum Yum Tree. Restaurant management wasn't for her, though, so she took a job in marketing. A few months later my dad needed a new HR director. Mandie had run HR for her dad's 700 employees in South Africa, so she accepted the position. After seven months we bought a condo. Even though we were in a tropical paradise, it's not like we had money to explore the other islands. In two years I went to Maui once. I went to the Big Island once on a time-share sales pitch.

We were pretty much flat broke. I started at $45,000 a year and then when I was promoted to general manager I got a raise to $55,000. And there were all the inflated costs of living in Hawaii. By comparison, I had made almost $100,000 as a pro athlete and had very few expenses.

When you're an athlete you pay for nothing. Your bikes are paid for, your hotels are paid for, your food's paid for, and your transportation's paid for. You earn frequent flier miles during the racing season and you can fly free in the offseason. It's all paid for. I was used to traveling everywhere: Australia, Costa Rica, Africa, Europe — you name it. It's hard, the training, to stay that fit as an athlete, but you have a lot of time to do a lot of cool things, too. On top of that, I had always prided myself on saving money, but now Mandie and I were draining our savings just to pay the bills every month.

The reality is when you leave professional sports you go from being essentially a rock star to being a nobody. It's a rough transition. So much of your job as a professional athlete is dependent on your own drive and abilities. There's a lot of luck involved, too, but ultimately whether you're going to be successful or not is up to you. In contrast, much of my career advancement in Hawaii was out of my control. And maybe with more patience it would have been different, but I felt like I wasn't making a difference at all, unless you count roach eradication.

As a manager, bonuses were based on cash flow, and in order to maximize his bonuses, the previous Yum Yum Tree manager had cut costs deeper than he should have, including eliminating pest control. It took me a while to figure out we had a massive infestation of German cockroaches: the scourge of the islands. It was so bad I can't believe the health department didn't shut us down.

I directed the night crew to spray insecticides, and I would come in the next morning and sweep up dead German cockroaches piled up 6 inches deep along the walls. One of our signature breakfast items was blueberry pancakes, and they were about half blueberries, half cockroaches. That's an exaggeration, but the pests were so incessant that they flattened themselves and tried to squeeze through the salt-air-hardened rubber gaskets on the doors of the reach-in refrigerators. It was awful.

Slowly, we started winning the Cockroach War, but there were battle setbacks, like the day a group of Marines came in to eat lunch and one of them politely asked to see the manager — me — after being served his salad.

"Excuse me, but I don't think he's supposed to be in my salad," he told me, pointing to a cockroach, marching through the iceberg lettuce.

I still cringe at the memory.

But, people ask me, "What about the 'aloha spirit,' that inclusive tradition that makes the islands such a laid-back, fun place to be?"

The "aloha spirit" is bullshit — a fake-friendly invention to encourage tourism, as disingenuous as resort luaus. Part of the beauty of Hawaii is that there are so many cultures — Korean, Japanese, Polynesian, and huge American military bases. But it's definitely not a melting pot. Everyone seemed to keep to themselves.

By coincidence, one of my Telluride classmates, Demian Brooks, was living in Oahu, too. Out of only thirteen students in my graduating class, two of us were on the same little island. Dem was a pilot with Northwest Airlines, based in Oahu.

One day Dem and I went surfing at Waikiki, the most popular beach for tourists in Honolulu — not exactly a locals hangout. We were paddling out to a beginner break when this big Hawaiian guy — some 270 pounds and all tatted up — started bearing down on us on a wave. We paddled like crazy to get out of his way. I narrowly dodged him, but Dem didn't, and he ran over the front of Dem's surfboard. The surfer could have made a small turn on the wave to avoid running Dem over, but he kept bearing straight at us.

I thought, *What a dick.*

Dem had lived in Hawaii for a few years, and he knew how these surf-turf wars played out.

He warned me: "Watch out. That guy's coming for us."

I couldn't believe he was serious. But sure enough, this guy was trying to fight us out on the ocean. He paddled back over to us and took a swing at Dem, barely missed him, and then flicked the front of his board, missing my friend's teeth by a few inches. His board could have cratered Dem's face. He also had a posse of fifteen or so friends not 100 feet away, but he could have taken us both out by himself. He looked like linebacker Junior Seau.

"Dude!" I yelled. "We're just learning. We weren't trying to mess up your wave!"

He paused for a second and gave me a good look-over, and it's possible the angry scars from my cycling face-plant made him think twice. I was still lean like a bike racer, and several people had actually asked me if I fought in the MMA. They thought I had the scrappy, scarred-up look of a fighter.

"You go Canoes!" he finally barked at us, which was a different surf break. That's the "aloha spirit" right there. Total bullshit.

Whenever the moon is full, however, I still remember one of my best times surfing. Dem and I decided we wanted to do a full-moon surf, and we took Hawaiian Junior Seau's advice and surfed at

Canoes. The waves were small but it was a perfect night: 80-degree water and the waves all to ourselves. It was surreal, surfing in the glow of the moon. We must have surfed for three hours that night.

The greatest thing that happened in Hawaii, though, was that our daughter, Mira, was born there on March 10, 1999. Mira means "aim" or "aspiration" in Spanish, and her arrival helped me line up my priorities. Mira also means "wonderful one" in Latin. We found the name in a baby name book and it fit for us.

When Mira was born I only took three days off from work. It just wasn't a situation where I could take more time off to get to know my daughter and help my wife with the transition. I had to work.

It was not a smooth start for our expanding family. Pretty little Mira had colic and screamed bloody murder for three months straight. Mandie was exhausted, and her family was halfway around the world. Without a support system, she had to navigate this new world of parenting on her own most of the time.

I was conflicted because I wanted to be home more, but my home life wasn't going well, either. Mandie and I were fighting a lot, and I think she was probably second-guessing all of her own life-changing decisions of the past year.

"I think the fact that I was pregnant with Mira made me realize I couldn't just quit," Mandie reflected. "Scott is not a quitter. He would have seen it through, but there were times when I felt like quitting. My mom actually told me, 'No, you are staying,' because she really knew that Scott was a good man from the start. Scott was very good at throwing me into the deep end. He was not pampering me. I hated him at the time for it because I thought he was just mean, but it was the best thing that could have happened to me because I did figure things out."

A cloud of unspoken regret hung over both my home life and my work life, especially when four months later my old team, Postal, won the Tour de France. Watching those guys on television riding into Paris, toasting with champagne, was very difficult for me. I was happy for my old teammates, but it was only a year-and-a-half since

I'd hung up my spurs.

Their bonuses for the Tour win were three times what I was making in a year. I knew they had all given in to doping, but I thought to myself, *What the fuck did I do?*

I felt trapped and hopeless and I had willingly put my family in this situation. When I'd heard Lance signed with Postal in 1998, a year after I'd left, I remember thinking it would have been fun to race with him. He was a former World Champion and he was coming back from cancer. And now they'd just won the fucking Tour de France.

As a new father, though, I began to take a longer worldview of things, beyond my own short-term goals. I had something more to work for than my own wins. I wanted to have a successful family. I knew it was my responsibility to make changes to my life and career if I didn't like the way things were going — for me, for Mandie, and now for Mira.

Despite my scorched-earth roach-assault, my hollandaise mastery, and soldiering through long shifts, the restaurants were struggling. The Hawaiian economy was not doing well. With a new baby, this should have been one of the happiest times for our growing family, but Mandie and I barely saw each other. When we did see each other, we fought. We were broke, and we were miserable.

"This isn't working," Mandie said of our arrangement with my dad.

"I owe him," I countered. "I need to help him turn the restaurants around."

"You don't owe him anything," she said. "You are an employee, not an owner!" She had grown up in a family business. She understood those distinctions better.

Truth was, I was not happy being stuck as a manager on the end of a broom. The thing that struck me was that it wasn't a partnership at all. I was just an employee drawing a paycheck like everyone else.

I understood I needed to learn the ropes, but my dad and I barely spent any time actually talking about the restaurant business. I wanted him to teach me about leases, personnel, franchises, etc. Instead of being in a restaurant-owning apprenticeship, I was operating a restaurant blindly on my own. In truth, I had progressed only a few rungs above being that Redondo Beach bus boy. My career was going in the wrong direction.

After a tough year, Mandie and I looked forward to a two-week trip to South Africa for the wedding of Mandie's brother Riaan and his fiancée, Debra. I worked extra days to justify an additional week off to add to the week I'd earned from a year of service. I left the restaurant in good hands, and Mandie and I were excited for the change of scenery and time to reconnect with her family.

Dad started selling off the Hawaii restaurants. He got some great deals on the individual sales, but I could see the business was shrinking, not growing. It wasn't the right place, or the right time, or the right business situation for me to make my mark.

Mandie and I agreed to bid aloha to Hawaii for good. Working in those restaurants for two years gave me some skills I could use later in my career, but if I had known what I was getting into, I never would have made that move.

At the same time I was trying to scrape together a living one blue-plate special at a time, my wife's family had a thriving business in South Africa. My father-in-law was the largest independent lumber contractor in the country. Mandie's mother adored me. She wanted us to move back there. I never really even investigated that as an option, and it probably wouldn't have been the right situation, but I should have at least looked.

My dad always tells me, "Get something to say no to," meaning keep your options open. I actually use that phrase all the time.

I might have joined the wrong family business.

Without that option of working with my dad, though, it's likely that I would have raced another year — and I know I would have succumbed to the pressure to dope.

Looking back, I know my biggest mistake when I left racing was not looking at other options. I should have done my homework, asked more questions and done more due diligence. I had made some assumptions about what my role in the business would be, but my dad and I weren't on the same page.

I started looking for alternatives, and when I told my dad I needed to get out, he was supportive and helped investigate ideas. I wouldn't necessarily want to relive that phase of my life, but my dad and I are much closer as a result of those two years. Today we have a healthy friendship and father-son relationship, and our time in Hawaii played a role.

But now what?

Chapter 14

GET YOUR HANDS DIRTY

*If you want the rewards, set your ego aside, roll up
your sleeves, and get to work.*

More deliberately this time, I weighed my career options. The list was longer. One: Go into investment banking. Two: Return to school and earn an MBA. Three: Open a pancake franchise in Salt Lake City. Four: Open a Carl's Jr. franchise in Colorado.

Of the four, I was leaning toward Carl's Jr. It had always been my favorite fast-food restaurant. On surf trips with my dad to San Onofre, we would stop at Carl's Jr. in San Clemente. My favorite sandwich was the barbecue chicken with waffle fries, which is still on the menu. Dad acquired the franchise in Hawaii and in Reno, Nevada.

I found out the franchise was just taking hold in Colorado, with a distribution center in Denver and a restaurant in Colorado Springs.

Plus, I missed Colorado and my family there. From growing up in Telluride, I knew outdoor recreation was a big part of Coloradans' lives. It was healthy, for both mind and body, to be active and outside more. It provided that elusive quality of life so many people search for. We could ski, hike, and ride our bikes. We could make a good life there for our family.

But where in Colorado? My first instinct was Durango, a

picturesque, tourism-driven town, but my little brother, Blake, said I should consider Grand Junction — the economy was diversifying and the college was growing. My initial thought was, *What? That redneck town? No way.*

The "Grand Junkyard" was what everyone in Telluride called it when we drove to the "big city" for dental appointments growing up. There used to be a large junkyard near the junction of the Colorado and Gunnison Rivers at the city's south entry. The fairgrounds were literally called "Uranium Downs" to boot. It didn't make a good first impression. I have grown to love the place and am as big a booster of Grand Junction as anybody, but at the time I was skeptical.

But from a business standpoint, the high-desert city seemed a good fit. It's large enough to support a Carl's Jr., it's also 4,000 feet lower in elevation than Telluride and 3,400 feet lower than Aspen, and it offers nearly year-round cycling opportunities.

My LA dad warned me it would take a while to get a franchise off the ground, but I didn't expect it would take two whole years. Needing cash flow, I went on the Monster board to see who was hiring and saw an ad for a financial planning job at an insurance company, AXA Advisors. My thought was I was just going to be with AXA for two years and then open the restaurant and move on.

I fell in love with financial planning, though, so I kept my licenses and split my focus. AXA was great to me, and the people were good people to work with. In financial planning, you eat what you kill — there is no base salary or safety net. My niche was working with small businesses and individuals and retirement planning.

I started with AXA in July, while I pursued the Carl's Jr. franchise. My taxable income that year was a whopping $4,000. To pay our bills, Mandie and I quickly blew through all our savings and built up $12,000 in credit card debt. We sold our condo in Hawaii, but when the real estate commission was factored in, we lost about $10,000 on the sale. We preferred to keep the condo as an investment property, but I didn't have a steady job where we could afford to take that mortgage risk. Our life was a continuing cash drain.

Despite my contentious experience working in restaurants for my dad in Hawaii, I was determined to try again, but this time on my own terms: as partners. I did all the legwork to secure the franchise and put a business plan together.

Dad came to Colorado and we did due diligence as a team. He lent me the start-up money, and I agreed to do the heavy lifting and not pay myself a salary as the operating partner. We had a clear-cut division of capital and labor. He invested the capital and I provided the labor. We agreed that if we later sold the restaurant, he would get his money first and we would split any remaining profits. We have actually sold both restaurants now but have kept one with a new franchisee as a long-term tenant. It's been a profitable partnership for both of us.

There was another reason I wanted to give the restaurant business another try. I'd witnessed that the restaurant business was a good investment because of the successful examples of my LA dad and his friends. And in the franchise business, it's nearly turn-key. There's a template in place with instant name recognition, plus a built-in advertising and marketing plan: an A- Easy Button.

What I failed to realize was that my dad and his friends put in a lot of time to get to where they were. These guys were in their 50s and 60s, not their 30s, like I was. They'd been at it awhile.

After two years, we finally opened our Carl's Jr. restaurant on July 14, 2002, with some of the highest volumes in the franchise system. Grand Junction was experiencing a natural gas boom, and we were booming along with it. We did $55,000 in sales the first week. The expectation is you'll lose about 50 to 60 percent of your first week's sales once the newness wears off and customers go back to their familiar dining habits. Weeks later I was still depositing stacks of cash 16 inches tall in the bank every day.

I'd had two years to plan for not only the first restaurant, but also a second, and I was on a roll. With Mandie working HR, accounting, and doing the franchise reporting, we broke ground on a second Carl's Jr. a week later and cleared $70,000 net profit in two months in the first restaurant. Sales were great, we owned the real estate, and I thought I'd be retiring at 45 with $20 million in the bank.

But I started pre-gaming my retirement a little too early. I wasn't paying enough attention to the operations. I was putting in 16-hour days for several months, but successful restaurants require those kinds of hours for longer than I kept up that pace. Plus, I overshot the mark. We were barely settling into the first restaurant when we had to hire and train staff for the second restaurant, which opened a mere twelve weeks later. I was focused on building the other restaurant rather than operational excellence.

Not only that, but we had another major expansion in the works. Our son, Marius, named for Mandie's brother, was born a few months later, on Sept. 13, 2002. Personally and professionally we were stretched too thinly and in too many directions. And to top things off, Mandie's mom died at 57 a few weeks after we opened the first restaurant. That was a blow that was painful and unexpected. She was actually planning to come to Colorado to help with Marius but had a massive aneurism a few weeks before she made the trip from South Africa.

I also made a series of poor hiring decisions that cost us dearly. It's amazing the business survived. I made a lot of mistakes. I know I cost us millions of dollars by running the restaurants so poorly.

There was a point when my dad told me in frustration: "You've got to get your hands dirty. You've got to get in there and run this business!"

So I quit my job as an advisor. I kept my licenses, but I dug into the day-to-day operations of the restaurants and slowly started turning them around. My dad was right. If I'd done that from the beginning, just made that commitment for a period of time, we'd have been in a different situation.

What I learned from that experience of opening two restaurants in as many months is that you have to be vigilant about your guests' experience — always. You constantly have to put yourself in your guests' shoes. For example, at one point we had an average of a 20-minute wait in the drive-through lane. No one's going to wait 20 minutes, no matter how good the burger is.

I had more to learn about personnel, too. I had a husband and wife who worked for me, with fifty years of Carl's Jr. experience between them. They seemed like great hires on paper, but we ended up having terrible turnover under their management.

With their experience, I thought I'd found the perfect managers. But what I learned from that was to check references. It took me a while to figure out they didn't treat people well. They knew the systems, they knew the numbers, and they knew the operations, but you can't scream at employees and call them worthless and expect them to be loyal. The couple was on their way to getting fired when they resigned to move to California.

After that experience, I instituted a firm No-Asshole Policy. If you're an asshole to customers, you're fired. If you're a shift manager and you yell at your crew, you're fired. That also applies to customers. If you're an asshole customer, you're not welcome back.

Around that time, there was an article in *The Wall Street Journal* about how one bad apple at work can spoil the whole bunch. I hung that clipping on the office wall, with appropriate warnings to would-be assholes highlighted.

Another thing I learned: Hire talent when it presents itself. Don't get caught back on your heels, needing to quickly replace someone when they quit or are fired. It's sort of like when you're in a bike race and you're thirsty. By that time it's too late. You're done. You need to drink before you're thirsty. We started a policy that anyone who applies for a job gets an interview.

We regularly scheduled interviews twice a week, on Tuesdays and Fridays, and if we found somebody who was promising, even if we didn't have a spot, we'd hire them. The results were amazing.

The other thing we've found is if you're not staffed properly, you get desperate to keep people you shouldn't try to keep.

In Hawaii, our best cook one year had refused to work Mother's Day. For a restaurant with a breakfast focus, Mother's Day is one of your biggest days of the year. You don't work for the NFL and say you don't want to play on a Sunday, and you don't work at a breakfast restaurant and say you don't want to work on Mother's Day.

I fired him, and it sent a message to the rest of the staff that no one is indispensable. But the reality is that nobody really gets fired. They, in effect, fire themselves through their behavior.

For about five or six years I was the general manger at one of the stores while I kept working at AXA. I didn't take my dad's admonition to get in there and get my hands dirty lightly.

One day, a member of the crew took me aside and whispered: "There's a problem. Somebody shit all over the women's restroom."

So I hurried toward the women's restroom, and it was like Hansel and Gretel's breadcrumbs trail, only with Hershey's Kisses of poop. They were in a line all the way to the toilet.

While I was in there cleaning, someone kept pushing and pounding on the door. It was The Pooper. She'd shit all over the entryway and all along the restaurant floor and was trying to get back in to finish the job. She wasn't even a guest in the restaurant.

It was crappy, in every sense of the word. That was a low point.

Here I was an Olympic athlete, a former professional athlete, with a degree from Cal, cleaning up some woman's shit in the bathroom, the hallway, and the foyer. It took me 40 minutes to clean the mess, it was that bad. That day I questioned my allegiance to the family business, for sure.

But attention to cleanliness and minding the small details paid off. It's the little things in a business that can have a big impact. At one point I asked the employees for a list of everything that needed to be fixed in the restaurants to have them in top condition. It was a little here and a little there, but it added up. Keeping everything ship-shape established a level of pride and professionalism in the staff. They extended that attention to detail to the way they conducted themselves at work. But in all businesses there are risk factors beyond your control.

The Great Recession hit us hard. The natural gas boom in Grand Junction went bust, to boot. We lost a third of our sales in the downturn. My dad compares coming back from that economic decline to turning around an aircraft carrier. It takes a long time and sustained, collective effort to turn around an aircraft carrier; it's not going to happen overnight. We fired all the engines, bowed our necks, and redoubled our efforts on customer service, restaurant cleanliness, and serving hot, fresh food. To lessen the leverage on the business, even when the restaurants were not cash flowing very well, we prioritized paying down debt.

My dad and I now have a great relationship and a great partnership. We've gone through some challenges together and learned from each other. I remember there was a period where he got ripped off — one of his restaurant managers stole a lot of money: $30,000.

We talked about that and I chastised him, "Dad, you've got to pay attention!"

I'm at a point in our relationship where I can listen to his criticism without getting my hackles up. The perspective I take now is that he's trying to look out for my best interest. I don't take it personally anymore.

From my upbringing and from working in the restaurant industry, I've gained perspective about the economic struggles many people face. That's made me more empathetic about the need for a living — and not just a surviving, — wage. I voted for a minimum wage increase in Colorado, and it barely impacted my bottom line. We all do better when we all do better. There is no societal reward from stinginess.

All in all, I'm happy with my life. You always wonder, *Is there more?* It's a hard balancing act to find personal and professional growth without losing sight of what's important. You want to be content, but not complacent. But there is a time in your life when you take and a time in your life when you give, and I'm in the phase of my life where I'm giving to my family, first, and to my community when I can.

I even reconnected with cycling through my involvement with Roaring Fork Cycling and Colorado Mesa University, where I served in a volunteer capacity as Cycling Director for the collegiate cycling team.

I try to teach young athletes to get out of their comfort zones, to not ride for second place but to race to win. You are going to lose more often than you win, but if you don't attack you will never put yourself in a position to win. Don't be satisfied with sixth place — it's okay if you finish sixth if you have given all you have, but don't aspire to be sixth.

What I emphasize with college athletes is the importance of hard work. There is a direct correlation between how much you study and the grades you get, and there is a direct correlation between how much you train and how well you compete. And it's not just how much you train, but how much you sacrifice while training. You can't just go out with your buddies for rides six days a week and joke around and bullshit. You have to push your boundaries. You have to suffer.

More recently, I've come to fully appreciate through engagements with the U.S. military how discipline and sacrifice don't just make the difference between winning or losing, or financially struggling or thriving, but between actual life or death. I've been invited several times to give keynote speeches at West Point celebrations. This was a first-hand introduction to the impressive operations of our military and how well it represents the range of American experience. The military is a robust cross-section of society, with diversity of gender, race, and social background, but despite their differences, all service men and women are unified by, and dedicated to, a common mission.

It is humbling beyond words to stand on stage, pause at the podium, and look around a room full of attentive, young cadets and realize they would sacrifice their lives for their country, for my family, for me. They are the real heroes, not athletes. It is immensely personally rewarding that my story is instructive to the character development of cadets.

One cadet came up to me after a presentation and asked for advice on physical conditioning, as he was preparing for Ranger school. We talked for 20 minutes about how to overcome physical discomfort. I think of him now and hope he has maintained strength, vigilance, and health. The military forges character through the greater stakes. I meet veterans, and I recognize the fraternity of men and women who have been bonded through common — sometimes horrific — experience.

More often, I'm invited to speak to young athletes. One event that stands out is the Collegiate Road Nationals in Ogden, Utah. I scanned the nearly 500 student athletes, including some from Cal, and had a flashback to when I was a 22-year-old college kid.

I thought about what cycling has meant to me and how education has broadened my life.

I recalled the earlier lesson I'd received about how education can open doors when I crossed paths after high school with the 18-year-old coal-mining kid from Kentucky. Education ensures options. And even if one path leads down a box canyon, having an education can provide other paths to choose from. Not everyone has those choices.

"Don't forget who is keeping your electric lights on while you are studying next year at Berkeley," my LA dad had told me near the end of our cross-country bike tour.

I didn't forget, and I am grateful.

I thought about my mom, who not only brought me into the world, but taught me how to navigate it.

I thought about my Telluride dad, who instilled in me independence and accountability.

As I spoke to those student-athletes in Ogden, I assured them they would be better men and women because of the time they spent racing their bikes. They would have learned about suffering, about sacrificing for others, and that while you may win or lose as an individual, there is a team of people helping you succeed. Those are life skills, not just skills needed to become a professional cyclist. Education provides options and opportunities, and I think the sport needs the collegiate program to thrive. I don't know what the path forward is to make this happen, but with attention and resources, collegiate cycling could grow and benefit student-athletes.

Too many young professional athletes feel they have one option, one shot, and they're desperate to do anything coaches and team doctors tell them to do. And when they're used up and spit out, they don't have anything to fall back on.

This issue is important to me, so I asked my old coach Chris Carmichael for his insight.

"I think we can encourage collegiate cyclists to have greater access into the pro ranks and also create some barriers so young talent doesn't get drafted into the pro ranks too early," he said.

"There has to be a minimum age," coach continued. "I think some of it is just level of maturity, which is important for them, and hopefully means they can go to college, race collegiately, and they know that they cannot be drafted into the pro ranks before 24-years-old, or whatever the minimum age is. And that way it creates a little bit of a barrier so you don't get a guy who is a really good talent at 20 coming in but just doesn't have the maturity yet. The physical maturity may be there, but the breadth of life experiences isn't. Better that they've seen other things so when they get to the pro ranks they have some education under their belt so if it doesn't work out they don't have to choose between cycling and education."

Even for the uber talented, the odds of going pro are against them, he explained. "Maybe 1 in 10,000 college cyclists is going to go pro, so worst-case scenario they get a degree and they've got skills. Sure, in college you may drink too much, stay up too late, and party too much, but you still have some structure and you have to do the work or you won't graduate. The racing calendar also lines up really well with the collegiate calendar. You could take a dozen of these college athletes and put them into the national program in Europe on summer, spring, or Christmas breaks. It's a way for college athletes to become professionals while staying in college."

I couldn't agree more. My years as a professional athlete were some of the best years of my life, but it's a short time span, in the big scheme of things.

If you're lucky, there's a lot more life to live.

Chapter 15

DON'T BE SILENCED

Muting the truth doesn't change the reality.

My Twitter bio reads: "Sometimes you have to stand up for the little guy — especially if you are the little guy."

In mid-August of 2013, I got a cryptic text message from a Colorado Springs number: "Hey Scott, this is Travis from USADA. If you have a minute I'd like to talk." I thought to myself, *Why would Travis Tygart want to talk to me?* I was skeptical so I replied, "Is this a joke? But if not, sure." I knew who Travis was: an attorney and the CEO of the United States Anti-Doping Agency — USADA. Travis was the pit bull who refused to be cowed by Lance Armstrong; it was he who slayed the King.

I hadn't been involved in cycling for over a decade and I was taken aback by his text. I didn't know why he would want to talk to me. A few minutes later my phone rang. After a few pleasantries he got straight to the point. He said: "I've been meaning to call you for some time. Your name came up again and again as part of our investigation into the USPS cycling team. It was unanimous and consistent that you were one of the few who said no to the culture of drugs. I am calling today to thank you for your strength of character and to ask you how you were able to do what so few were able to do: say no. It's athletes like you who we at USADA are fighting for, to give guys like you a fighting chance."

He went on to tell me that my former teammate, Tyler Hamilton, was publishing a book about the doping culture and that I was mentioned several times. The book, *The Secret Race*, was due to come out in a few weeks, but he had an advance copy. Travis asked if he could read a passage to me. In the passage, I discussed my reasons for leaving the sport after being presented with performance-enhancing drugs for the first time by our team doctor:

"I thought about it a long time. A tough decision, and in the end, I didn't take the pills and I quit at the end of the year. My heart wasn't in it. What made the difference for me is that I was already twenty-eight; I'd had a good career; I had some options for going forward in my life. I went into business, have done pretty well. Even so, I've wrestled with that decision for fourteen years. I don't blame people who did it in the least — I get why they did it. I mean, look at Tyler —look at how well he did in that world! It's been strange watching that from afar, wondering what might have been, if I'd made a different choice."

Travis said that passage was the most powerful statement he had ever read about the beauty of sport and the power of clean athletes. I was stunned by this recognition. This simple exchange would start a tsunami of media requests from around the world: NBC, CNN, Sky Sport, NPR, and newspapers from Australia to Europe to South Africa. They all wanted to hear the story of the guy who said "No" — the Anti-Lance.

With the unraveling of the pervasive USPS doping scandal, people often ask, "How could they have gotten away with it for so long?" The answer is simple: omertà.

Omertà has its origins in Corsica and Sicily in Italy. It is a code of honor that places an importance on solidarity, silence, and a refusal to cooperate with authorities. Many crimes committed by the mafia will go unsolved for decades because of omertà. In exchange for silence, the mafia ensures that the perpetrator's family is well cared for. Break the code of silence, though, and you're excised for good.

Omertà may have even deeper roots in cycling than in the mafia. Whereas the mafia typically would have an informant inside the police department and perhaps a judge on the payroll, in cycling the entire sport — from the governing bodies to race promoters to team managers — is filled with former professional riders. Imagine how difficult any crime would be to prosecute if former members of the mafia controlled the police department, the judicial system, and the district attorney's office. That is what we are faced with in cycling: Today's team managers, race promoters, and governing bodies are filled with yesterday's professionals. And many, if not all, were dopers.

During the 2014 USA Pro Cycling Challenge I met with Bob Stapleton, the Chairman of the USA Cycling Board, to talk about the current state of the sport and share ideas as to how to move forward after the shellacking cycling took from the Lance Armstrong fiasco. Bob recently had become the chairman of the board and seemed interested in taking USA Cycling in a different direction. He also was at one time the owner of one of the most successful programs in professional cycling: Team HTC Columbia.

We had lunch in Aspen prior to the start of the race and discussed the possibility of my becoming involved with the governing board for USA Cycling. Bob asked me to put together a CV and to join USA Cycling as a member. He indicated that I would be a "controversial" member but that with my background I could provide some needed insight and be a valuable addition to the board. Eventually, the conversation turned to funding and we discussed Thomas Weisel. Weisel was on the USA Cycling Foundation Board of Directors and had been the owner of the USPS Cycling team when I raced for them. His son, Brett, and I were close friends from Cal. I had been a groomsman in Brett's wedding in 1996.

Bob asked me point-blank, "What is your relationship with Weisel?" I told him that I honestly didn't know. Brett hadn't returned any of my calls or texts over the past year, so I suspected that he was uncomfortable with my stance on doping and cheating.

Bob implied that there was a sense of urgency, so I joined USA

Cycling that night and sent Bob my CV a few days later. A week or so went by with no response, so I pinged him again. Still nothing. A few weeks later I sent Bob a third follow-up. Still nothing. Lance and I went riding during this time and we talked about my potential as a board member. He thought it weird that Bob had not even responded. I was pretty sure that Bob was ghosting me and that I had been blackballed from USA Cycling. I wasn't sure, however, if it was because of my relationship with Lance or if it had something to do with Thom Weisel. Finally, I texted Brett, point-blank, why he never returned my calls or texts and he sent a cryptic reply: "your quotes in books and the media." That was it. No explanation, no follow-up call, nothing.

I was stunned. I considered Brett one of my closest friends. We did not see each other much, but I loved him. He was one of the most genuine people I had ever met. But I found out he felt I had betrayed him and his family. I thought: *What the fuck? Omertà.* The cruelest irony is that I was one of the few who ever had anything good to say about his dad in cycling. I never had any indication that he knew about what was happening with the doping program. It always appeared to me as if the Europeans tried to hide the doping from Thom. He was the sponsor and the money behind the team, but he didn't call the doping shots. Quite frankly I had always thought Thom's support of cycling was good for the sport. Granted, I was only on the team for a year, but that is what I felt. I asked Darren Baker about it, and he said that he felt the same way.

Awhile back, Brett called me out of the blue. He wanted to apologize. I listened politely and have accepted his apology, but we'll never be close again.

A few months later the Union Cycliste Internationale (UCI) published the results of Cycling Independent Reform Commission (CIRC), their year-long investigation into the doping practices within the sport during the late '90s and the first part of the new millennium. They published a list of the riders and former riders who had agreed to be interviewed for the report. I was one of the few who agreed to have my name published. A reporter from CNN interviewed me about the report. One of his questions had to do with my involvement with USA Cycling. He was stunned when I mentioned that I had no involvement and that I had not heard from them. In fact, the title of the column was, "Scott Mercier: The Anti-Lance Armstrong is still cycling's outsider." In the column I mentioned that it felt like a continuance of the omertà. After the column was published, Bob left me a voicemail indicating that he wanted to talk.

I wanted to learn more background on Bob before I spoke to him again, so I called George Hincapie. George had ridden and worked for Bob for several years. In George's opinion, Bob was a straight-shooter, and George was confident this was just a misunderstanding. He said, "I think so many issues like this could be cleared up with a phone call, speaking directly." It was advice I took to heart and still do. Confronting issues directly is always the best tack.

My eventual conversation with Bob was uncomfortable, but at least we came to a resolution. Bob told me he was disappointed with what I'd said in the CNN story. He assured me I had not been blackballed from USA Cycling. It was a misunderstanding, he assured, about the sense of urgency in respect to the decision about the USA Cycling board.

"Bob, you gave me the impression there was a sense of urgency," I said. "I followed up with you several times and heard nothing. What was I supposed to think?" He assured me my concerns were misguided but conceded he could understand why I thought I'd been shut out. I realized Bob was a volunteer trying to remake and rebuild an entire sport in the U.S. He was trying to make it relevant again and get cycling back on a sound growth trajectory.

USA Cycling does seem to be trying to move on from the past. In 2021 I was invited to a WebEx with dozens of former athletes and coaches and the director went to great lengths to explain his vision for both the competitive aspect of cycling in America and his goal to get more kids on bikes. Maybe cycling in America is turning the corner.

Win True

Chapter 16
DON'T ASSUME ANYTHING

Without direct communication our brains work overtime to fill the void. That's how hard feelings get a foothold.

The Denver Post Ride the Rockies is a hugely popular, noncompetitive summer bicycle tour in Colorado that raises money for The Denver Post Community Foundation. The foundation supports programs that benefit children, the arts, literacy, education, and human services. Some 2,000 cyclists ride for six to seven days, with a different route each year cresting Colorado's challenging mountain passes.

In 2013, the route was from Telluride to Colorado Springs. As an Olympic cyclist who grew up in Telluride, I was invited to be one of the VIPs to accompany participants on the Prologue Ride. For a $2,500 donation, fifty riders could "rub elbows for two days with local celebrities and cycling legends," according to the sales pitch by ride organizers.

Those cycling legends included Nelson Vails, Ron Kiefel, George Hincapie, Chris Carmichael, and me. George's company, Hincapie Sportswear, based in Greenville, South Carolina, was the official jersey sponsor of the event.

I'd heard George was going to be there, so before the June ride I emailed him: "I know you're going to be in Telluride. I hope you're doing well. Maybe we can catch up."

I was pretty sure Big G wasn't happy with me for a couple of comments I had made, so I thought I would extend an olive branch. In 2011, I was interviewed in VeloNews about doping on Postal and I mentioned that George and I had discussed it over coffee in 1997. And after the USADA Reasoned Decision regarding the USPS doping scandal, I read that George apparently asked Frankie Andreu to rein in his wife Betsy's public comments about doping in cycling.

For some reason, that really grated on me. I don't know Betsy, but I thought it was over the line for Big G to go after another teammate's wife — particularly when she was telling the truth.

In any case, reading that really pissed me off and I tweeted something like this: "Shame on you, George, you don't attack Frankie's wife."

In retrospect, I shouldn't have done that. I don't know what happened between George and Frankie. I've been attacked many times by Betsy myself. It always makes me chuckle, too. She attacks the clean guy who willingly gave up his spot on U.S. Postal rather than become a doper. My decision to leave the team opened up a spot for her doper husband, Frankie. I've always found it ironic how she attacks me for not going public about doping on Postal. It's also incredibly hypocritical for her to have attacked former Postal soigneur Emma O'Reilly when Emma decided to accept Lance's apology and forgive him. What Betsy also fails to understand is that while I did go public, I only had direct knowledge about myself. Lance and I were not teammates on Postal. Betsy and Frankie went through what must have been an unbelievably tough time, but I don't think that gives her the right to attack anyone who may have a differing point of view.

I heard nothing back from George before the Ride the Rockies.

Friday night at the welcome reception, George was standing with some of his cronies and I walked over to him.

"Hey, George, how are you doing?"

"Hey, Scott," he said coldly, and turned his back on me.

He would not say another word to me. This is a guy who was my roommate training for the Olympics and on the Postal team in Girona. We'd spent a fair amount of time together. Many view him as Cancer Jesus' Judas. The final straw that broke the camel's back for Lance Armstrong was George Hincapie's testimony. Lance made George millions. Don't get me wrong; Big G was a great cyclist, but Lance really opened his career for him.

I found it ironic for a guy who's asking the public to forgive him, who took down Lance, and whom Lance forgave, to shun me — the guy who did things the right way. You can't ask for forgiveness if you aren't willing to offer forgiveness.

That's how I felt at the time, but I'd later find out there was more to the story. A lot of friendships were strained following the doping scandal fallout as events played out publicly in media interviews. And then there's social media, where everyone has an opinion and there is zero filter. Our friendship took some hits in this media maelstrom. Emotions ran high on all sides of the issue. They still do.

Before the Ride the Rockies reception, I'd decided that if George was going to be gracious to me, I was going to wear a Colorado Mesa University cycling kit for the Prologue Ride. But I also had a RideClean kit that I was going to wear if he was a dick. My RideClean kit came from Doug Loveday, an old racing buddy, now living in Tucson, Arizona. Doug started a clean athletics program in 2006.

It's pretty poignant that here was one of the titans of American cycling — George did 17 tours — a rider I lived with in Girona and started racing with in 1992, a rider who took a completely different path and decided to turn his ass into a pin cushion, and he turned his back on me when I extended an olive branch to him, twice. So I thought, *Okay, you want to make a distinction between the two of us? I'll happily do that.*

The morning we were getting our bikes and gear together for the Prologue Ride, Peter Stubenrauch, whom I'd recently been riding with in Moab, sent me a text, saying: "I got 20 bucks if you get a photo of you and George together with that RideClean kit."

I thought, *That's the easiest twenty bucks I'll ever make.*

I asked a friend on the ride, Joel Cantor, to go up to George and say, "George, I want a picture of the two of you old teammates."

I knew George would not say no to a client. Joel had paid to be part of the Prologue ride. I was right. After I sent Peter the photo, he responded, "Look at the shit-eating grin on your face and look at George."

George had a painful look on his face, like he would have preferred to be anywhere in the world rather than posing for a photo with me in a RideClean kit. His dismissal of me was so obvious that even Telluride locals noticed. This was my town, where I grew up, and people were going up to my mother and saying George was a coward — that he wouldn't even shake my hand.

Chris Carmichael also would barely talk to me at that time. Chris' son, who was about 13, also was there for the ride. I told him his dad was one of the best coaches I ever had, that I became a much better cyclist with Chris' guidance.

We started the scenic, 50-mile Prologue Ride from Telluride to Ouray. There were some people — family and friends of my parents — who came out to cheer me on.

They clanged cowbells and yelled, "Go, Scott! Go, Scott! It was all in fun. It wasn't a race. They called it a no-drop ride, meaning that we would stop and wait for any stragglers. My brother, his wife, and my nephew were up by Dallas Divide watching everybody ride by. The weather was perfect, 82 degrees, and it was an easy ride: one small climb sandwiched between two downhill stretches.

The only hard section, and it wasn't that hard, was coming to the top of Dallas Divide, a saddle 8,983 feet in elevation between the San Juan Mountains and the Uncompahgre Plateau. George stayed at the front with the leading riders. Eventually it got down to just four of us out front. George may have been humorless the night before, but he said something to one of the prologue riders, a Realtor from Telluride, that I thought was really funny.

Typically, when you're riding side by side, you keep the front of your wheels together so you're next to each other. A half-wheeler, however, is a guy who always has to be a half-wheel ahead. The half-wheeler is, quite frankly, despised.

It's just some passive-aggressive thing, like the dude who gives you the short grab when he shakes your hand. Basically, they're trying to assert their dominance — that they're stronger than you and can stay ahead of you. If you accelerate to keep your wheel even with the half-wheeler, he's going to accelerate to keep his wheel ahead of yours, and eventually it will turn into a flat-out race.

There's always that one guy who wants to test the pro, and usually you'll let this guy — you know, the weight-lifter type guy — half-wheel you. Typically, in training camps you get these VIP guests who come along on rides, whether it's the publisher from VeloNews or Bicycling Magazine or some of the sponsors.

If you keep your wheel even with him, he'll keep accelerating, and you can watch your speedometer rise. You'll be cruising along at 18 miles an hour, and then you increase to 20 and then 22 and then 25, and eventually the half-wheeler reaches a point where he can no longer maintain that speed, but you still can, so he's going to end up blowing. You're basically sending the half-wheeler a message — *know your place* — and if he doesn't comprehend what you're doing, he just thinks you're racing him.

I'm not even sure if the half-wheeler is aware of what he's doing, but usually when anyone tries to half-wheel a pro, it ends badly. Plus, it's just bad form. If you're hitting balls with Roger Federer, you don't try and sneak one down the line real hard.

So this guy was half-wheeling George, who was a little overweight by cycling standards (meaning he's healthy!), but he'd ridden the Tour the previous year and he'd been a pro for a long time. He was still very fit, and this guy, the half-wheeler, he kind of did an attack. He'd been half-wheeling the whole time and now he was attacking. Only it wasn't much of an attack; it was more of a slight acceleration off the front.

We picked up the speed to catch him. George looked over at the half-wheeler and said, "Is that all you got?" which I thought was hilarious.

I was sitting comfortably on Big G's wheel and thought to myself,

No ... I have a lot more. I was honestly hoping he'd try to open it up. There was no way I was going to let him drop me. And worse for George was that the whole group saw us ride up the road: the Doper and the RideClean guy.

As I think now about my bitterness toward Big G at Ride the Rockies, if I am honest with myself, it really didn't have much to do with George himself, or even with my disdain for doping. I don't think he was the hypocrite. I think I was. To be quite frank, there was a certain amount of jealousy on my part. I was jealous of the racing career he had and, despite his own admitted doping, the esteem he enjoys and the business success he continues to have in the cycling world.

I didn't feel that way toward other riders — not even Lance. It's more personal, and more relatable, with George. It's raw with him. I see parallels between his cycling career and mine, and it makes our different outcomes all the more glaring, by comparison.

Our professional careers started about the same time, and then we had all these intersections: riding on the National Team, roommates preparing for the 1992 Olympic team, and then five years later as Postal teammates. I think my bitterness toward him was my frustration with the sport that I took out on him, fairly and unfairly — probably a little of both.

I've come to realize that in this debacle of doping, nobody is perfect. We have all made mistakes, and we all are hypocritical in our own ways. I think some of my frustration with George was justified, but most of it probably was not, because if I'm going to acknowledge that doping was institutionalized and systemic, how can I unfairly single out one guy who I just happened to be very close to at a certain time in my life?

George, by any measure, had an enviable career. He was a three-time U.S. National Champion. He won a mountain stage of the Tour de France and shepherded Lance and Postal to seven consecutive Tour victories. But we were similar with our potential, I believe. George was certainly a much better bike-handler and could read a race well, but I was a better climber and had more raw power. So when I think of George, on the one hand he has enjoyed the fruits of his labor — I mean the guy worked his ass off — but there is no question that he also benefitted from his partnership with Lance and the competitive edge doping gave both of them.

Still, today George is greatly respected within the sport. I can't argue that he is not doing good things for the sport. Is he enriching himself? Probably, but that's the way life works and a lot of kids have opportunities because of his involvement in the sport. There is absolutely nothing wrong with him capitalizing on his name and his career — this is a capitalistic society, after all.

I've got to recognize that, as well.

When I think back to Ride the Rockies, I feel he had been personally hurt by what I said about him. I didn't want to hurt George's feelings. I honestly do think he's a very kind person. For me to tweet what I did about him was, quite frankly, chickenshit.

I should have just called him and talked one-on-one. If I had, we never would have had this misunderstanding in the first place.

As it turned out, it wasn't even the tweet that he was upset about. It was a CNN interview, and what I said wasn't directed at him. But I'll let Big G explain his interpretation himself.

"Simply for me, it was something you said in the press," George said. "I really didn't care about anything else, but one particular statement you said really hurt me. It was a CNN interview where you said, 'If I was George I don't know how I could wake my kids up in the morning and look them in the eye knowing that I was a lying cheat'— something like that."

Ouch. I understood why he was angry. Family is personal. George explained more.

"The statement involved my children," George said, "and it just destroyed me. It was one of the worst things I had ever read, and I have read some bad stuff. It was questioning my ability to parent — what I teach my children. For me, it was over the line. I was just so mad. I didn't care about anything else that was said. A lot of it was true, but that was not true, and it really hurt. To me, even if I hate someone, I would never go out to the press and say, 'Hey, that guy is an asshole, cheater, liar.' I would much prefer to say it to their face."

There was plenty of blame to go around, but we mended our fences.

"Now that I have spoken to you, I kind of see where you were coming from," George said. "We have different opinions. You made different choices than I did. I was jealous of you, really, that you had other options. You had a college degree and a job to go home to, and I always felt that I had nothing else. I had everything invested in trying to make it in cycling, and I felt as though it was my only choice to make those decisions. I kind of felt jealous that you had options to make another choice."

Once we talked in person, we sorted out the confusion. It's amazing the changes you can make with the troubled relationships in your life when you air things out, face to face.

"I feel lucky that I have gotten my relationship back with you," George said. "I was so mad at you, and I'm sure you were mad at me, but it is funny what happens sometimes when you just talk to somebody and communicate with them, which is what we did. I feel like our differences have been settled, whereas if you read some interviews from some people, we are fortunate."

For the record, this was the quote George read at CNN. Even though I was talking about myself, not George, as a father, I understand his protective instinct: "I wouldn't trade places with George Hincapie and his millions, or Tyler Hamilton and his Olympic medal. My wife said to me, 'Imagine you're coming home and telling your son and daughter Daddy is a liar, a cheat and a fraud. You don't have to do that.' So I feel good about the decision I've made. I wouldn't change anything."

As I re-read this interview, I can see how George personalized what was said. My wife had watched me agonize and struggle after I left the sport. I watched my former team, a team I left on my own volition, go on to dominate the sport.

Mandie knew the great experiences that they had — and what they earned from them. I missed all of that because of my decision to leave the sport. But what she said had nothing to do with George or Tyler or anyone else. She merely was saying to me that while I missed some great things, I also was spared a difficult conversation with my kids.

I didn't have to have a conversation like the one Lance had with his kids. I missed a lot, but I was also spared a lot of pain. I knew what George and the others were doing to achieve their success, but I still respected the work they put in to achieve those goals. You don't just put a needle in your ass and suddenly become a great athlete.

That has been lost in this story, as well: the work and the dedication required to succeed. George was — in my mind — a consummate professional. He was, and remains, a gentleman.

As one of the few people who chose not to dope in the high levels of professional cycling, I'm an attractive interview for media. I understand that, and I'm upfront about telling my story. I care about the sport of cycling, and I want to see it cleaned up, for riders and for fans. The sport deserves that.

I stand behind what I say, but what I say is not always interpreted the way I meant it. That's the nature of the beast. I've largely had good experiences with professional media — CNN, VeloNews, national and local newspapers, The Telegraph, PBS, Cycling News, the Today show.

I've had less-pleasant experiences with some bloggers and with social media, where many people — who don't know me and don't really understand the issues — often feel free to lob insults in my direction. There is more of an emotional impulse there. Put anything out there and it will get pounced on, and it's really hard not to punch back.

My LA dad once told me to never get in a pissing contest with a skunk. He was right. Win or lose, both sides come out smelling the same way.

I'm kind of boycotting social media now. I deleted it from my phone. If I want to go on Twitter or Facebook, I'll do it from my laptop once or twice a week. Otherwise, I find it becomes addictive, where I check it five or six times a day to see who re-tweeted this or that.

Nobody's without fault. People are not all good or all bad — they are more complex than that. But I believe most people are worthy of redemption, of second chances, of learning from their mistakes, paying their penance, and having the chance to make better decisions going forward. How could that be a bad thing?

Good riders were honorably loyal — and good riders were loyal for dishonorable reasons. There was ambition in professional cycling, there was greed, there was lying, there was cheating, and there was jealousy. Very few people came out without something to regret.

George added his perspective.

"People have lives outside of cycling," he said. "They have families and jobs and they don't just want to keep focusing on something that happened twenty years ago. They want to focus on the future and focus on their family's future, so when you read about the stories popping up again it's like, " *'Okay, enough already. Let's just move on.'* "

In some ways, I'm glad I don't make my living in the sport. George still has to live in that bitterly divided world, where everyone has an opinion and, thanks to social media, everyone has a forum. It's easy for me to just look at the good things he has — the money, the fame — but there is somebody slamming him every day about something. Every day somebody is making some rude comment about him.

If I have something to say, I'll give him a call. Or better yet, I'll invite him to go for a ride.

It was on bikes, after all, that we were always able to see eye-to-eye.

Chapter 17

IT'S NOT ALWAYS SUPPOSED TO BE FUN

What really differentiates people is how much they are willing to suffer. The struggle leads to the fun.

Eventually, I came full circle with another old cycling friend: Coach Chris Carmichael. Two years after that tense Ride the Rockies Prologue experience in 2013, Chris and I had another chance to reconnect.

Although George and I had patched things up, Chris and I hadn't. I still didn't know why he was snubbing me.

In 2015 Ride the Rockies started where I lived, in Grand Junction, for a 465-mile ride from June 13–20. But the VIP Prologue ride commenced from Gateway Canyons, a resort in red-rock canyonlands an hour southwest of Grand Junction owned by Discovery Channel founder John Hendricks. Invited special guest riders included Ron Kiefel, Nelson Vails, Allen Lim, Chris Carmichael, and me.

We stayed two nights at Gateway Canyons. It was personally satisfying, and I felt fortunate to once again be involved with the Prologue. The Prologue ride was from Gateway Canyons, through Unaweep Canyon, to Colterris Winery, which is perched above the Colorado River in the Palisade wine country. It was a one-way route. The plan was to shuttle riders back to the resort for dinner.

I saw Chris the night before the Prologue.

"Do you want to ride back together?" he asked, instead of catching the shuttle. It was a 55-mile ride from the winery back to the resort.

"You bet," I said. We'd previously always had a good relationship. I give him full credit for coaching me up from a green go-getter to a more powerful, confident rider. He helped me discover how to maximize my power. I thought a long ride together would be a great way to reconnect. Our conversation circled back to our early days together, when he coached me at camps.

"You were this guy that was dumb as an ox but had this massive motor — just totally green," he recalled. We talked about the team time trial meltdown at the Olympics, too.

Old competitors never change. Turns out we're both on Strava: a website on which runners and cyclists post their best times on various routes. It's a way to keep track of your personal bests and to invite a little friendly competition. I didn't know there was a King of the Mountain route between Gateway and Colterris Winery on Strava, but apparently there is.

Chris uploaded his time first and won a King of the Mountain on a segment that day, but I uploaded my time two days later. He got an email from Strava saying I stole his KOM, which is kind of funny. He's no slacker, though. He is coaching, and he rides a lot, but he's not very fast. His business, CTS, for Carmichael Training Systems, is headquartered in Colorado Springs, with other locations in California, Arizona, North Carolina, and Mexico City.

He probably does 15,000 miles a year on the bike. Obviously the Lance fallout and the economy impacted his business pretty negatively, but it sounds like it is doing pretty well now.

Chris has an interesting story about how his own professional cycling career ended, and why he started coaching at a young age. "I broke my femur a few months after racing in the Tour de France the first time as part of the first U.S. team and that was eventually the end of my cycling career. I was backcountry skiing on Mount Shasta. It was in November — the first snow — and we went a long way and then hiked in a long way and then we were going to do some telemarking and I just sort of had a freak incident and had a bunch of injuries. That was '86. It was before Internet and cellphones."

He would never be the same, he explained. "I did come back to racing, but every season when it would be over I would have to have more surgery. There was too much pain and too much rehab. I was doing that for three or four years and it was like, *Okay, there is nothing more I can do.* I got asked to do some coaching with some development riders at the Olympic Training Center and I had never really envisioned myself doing that. Once I did, though, it was just something I loved and felt like I had an aptitude for it. I could articulate to the athletes what the expectations were and the best practices and approaches. I like to believe I am a better coach than I was an athlete. I guess I would say my success as a coach has been greater than my success as an athlete. Not that I necessarily had a bad career as an athlete, but I have worked with some amazing athletes and played a role in their success at some level, so I am very fortunate that I got into coaching, even though it was by the end of my own career. But that door closed and a new one opened and it has led to greater success and satisfaction for me."

Celebrating the success of the athletes you coach is a step removed from enjoying your own success, but it has its own rewards. "There are two athletes that I feel like I kind of founded in my coaching career at U.S. Cycling: both you and Darren Baker. There were other athletes I feel like I played a role in their development, like George Hincapie and Bobby Julich, but these guys were already established. They were really good junior cyclists and already doing really well. They were already on the National Team when I came in, but you and Darren were two athletes who just had big engines. Nobody had really heard of you before and I saw you in different races domestically and then got you in the National Team program and you just started shining."

I was struck by how remarkable it was that the two athletes he was most proud of developing — Darren and me — had been the clean riders who left Postal rather than dope. For coach, though, he just remembered our potential.

"You know, Darren was a great road cyclist, a really good climber. He had a really good attitude, too. He was easy and adaptive to different situations. We took him to Mexico — he had no problems adapting there. We took him to Europe — no problems adapting there in a different environment. He was a really good cyclist and I remember talking to him, I don't know a year into his pro racing career, and I was a little surprised he had not had some good performances. At that stage they were just sort of dull, nothing was popping. He said he had gotten sick. He did not mention to me anything about doping, but I just remember being really surprised because I had thought, *Once he gets into the pro races, with as hard as those races are and with those climbs, he will have something that will shine and he will surprise some people,* but it just never happened."

And then he got to me and my late start in professional racing as a college graduate among hungry teenagers.

"You were in there. You had this big engine. You could ride all day at a hard level. You were a big guy so you were strong on the flats but also light and lean so you climbed well. You were learning the craft of racing, like being in the peloton and those types of things, because you were just so raw to it. That was starting to come, and if you had started three or four years younger, I think you could have been easily making the transition to road racing. You were probably somebody we would have been putting on the Olympic Road Race Team, and then 1996 as well."

And that thing that was bugging him about me, that made him standoffish in 2013? Turns out he was offended by some of my comments in a Colorado Springs newspaper article that made it seem, to him, that I was giving Lance an unfair amount of credit for his coaching success.

"It was because there was an article that my hometown newspaper wrote about me that was not very flattering and you had some quotes in there that I was surprised by," he explained.

"The vast majority of everything you said in that article was supportive; there was just one thing that I was like, *Jeez, Scott, you made it sound like all I did was slap Lance's name on this company and we had all of this money rolling in.* I think you said: 'Look, Chris was a very good coach, I never saw any indication of doping — he never brought that to me or never had any inclination of it or anything like that.' But there was a quote in there — and it is hard to know what gets taken and misrepresented and things like that — but about, oh, you know, something to the effect that I had made so much money because of Lance's success, and that irritated me."

Lance's meteoric success and then falling star impacted our coach for good and for bad. What I said to a Colorado Springs reporter struck a raw nerve.

"Lance was an athlete that I worked with on the National Team basically for 20 years," Chris explained. "Sometimes I was more involved, sometimes less involved, but I always felt that I was a positive influence on his cycling career. You know I never gave him drugs — performing-enhancing drugs — never encouraged him, never saw them, never transported, never any of that. Did I know he was doping? I think it would be silly to think otherwise, but it also was something like the vast majority of people in pro cycling he was competing against: Gianni Bugno, Bjarne Riis, etcetera. Was I pretty sure those guys were doping? Absolutely. Was I pretty sure Lance was doping? Absolutely."

And here's where the business connection occurred, which I had commented on.

"I gave Lance some stock in my company to be able to use his name and image, and we have been in business for fifteen years, and we were one of the first doing this," Chris said of the sponsorship arrangement. "Lance was very helpful in the success of CTS. Absolutely. But that did not come for nothing, and also that was not the only thing that could make our company successful."

On that three-hour ride, Coach and I were able to talk out our differences and repair our relationship.

"When you have a conflict, when you respect the person and have a friendship with them, you need to talk about it," Chris said. "Either you come to a resolution that you both feel okay about, or you don't, but at least you brought it to the other person's attention, and you made them aware, and you are sort of both man enough to discuss it. I really appreciated being able to do that with you at the last Ride the Rockies and I think we both understand each other and continue to respect each other."

It wasn't one-sided. Chris came to understand my point of view, as well.

"I also understood your position on some of the things you were going through in the midst of all of this, and I think you are right. There is sort of that collateral damage that keeps rolling. You said something the other day when we rode together — you said there have really been no winners in this thing and I kind of thought about it and was like, *God, you are really kind of right.* I think ultimately, hopefully, the winners are the people who are in there now who have an opportunity where you don't have to face it; it is just not part of something you have to face. You are one of the few who raised your hand and said, 'I don't want to do that.' It takes remarkable courage and strength. If more people would have done that it would have changed the nature of the sport."

I remember a valuable lesson coach taught me. We were doing interval training at the Olympic Training Center and one of the cyclists said, "This is not fun."

Chris stopped the workout and said: "This is the National Team. We are training for the Olympics. It is not supposed to be fun."

That still sticks with me: "It is not supposed to be fun." I think that's part of what's missing in our work ethic in our society.

Rather than work hard, people want to do what's fun. But suffering is still part of the journey that leads to success. To get where you want to be in any endeavor — if it's music, for example, then you are going to play until your fingers bleed — sometimes it is not going to be fun. The journey of perfecting your craft, and seeing your progress, is fun and rewarding. It is rewarding to achieve a level of excellence.

What really differentiates people is how much they are willing to suffer, and it is no fun to suffer. Whether it's in a relationship, or music, or athletics, or academics, it is not supposed to be fun all the time. But the end result can be fun. The suffering and perseverance lead to the fun.

Ride the Rockies in 2015 also invited me to give a 30-minute speech after the first stage over Colorado National Monument, which I could see from my front yard. The theme of my speech that night was "Win Clean." My former teammate, Ron Kiefel, introduced me. Even after a day of hard riding, some 200 people filed into the auditorium, paid attention, and asked lots of questions afterward. They asked about Lance, of course — I guess people will always be curious about him — but they also wanted to know how I had developed my moral compass. I showed some photos from my racing days and ended with talking about the choices we make in life, the forks in the road. I got a five-minute standing ovation.

Lance did not have an official role in Ride the Rockies, but a friend of his was riding and asked him to ride a stage with him, so Lance did. The friend is Tim League, of Austin, Texas, founder of Alamo Drafthouse Cinema, a chain of movie theaters that served high-end food, beer, and wine. Mandie and I had Lance and Tim over for dinner at our home. Lance stayed with us. We put him up in Marius' room while our son was away at Boy Scout camp.

Before Marius left, I gave him a heads-up that Lance would be staying in his room for a night. Marius was just starting to get into cycling, and I thought he'd think it was cool that Lance would be staying in his room. Marius was unimpressed, and he had a condition.

"Dad," he said, seriously, "Make sure he sleeps with his pants on!" He didn't want anyone — not even Lance Armstrong — sleeping naked in his bed.

The little dude is developing some healthy boundaries.

Win True

Chapter 18

OWN THE CONSEQUENCES

Integrity is highly valued because sometimes doing the right thing will come at a personal cost. Do it anyway.

I suppose that no story about cycling in the '90s could be complete without some mention of Lance Armstrong. Lance and I raced together in the early '90s, but we were never close friends. Perhaps even teammates is too strong of a word, but that's technically what we were when we raced together on the 1992 Olympic team and also the 1994 World Championship team in which I was selected to ride the time trial and to help him defend his title in the road race. I wouldn't say we were peers — he was always better than I was — but acquaintances.

The first time I raced with Lance was in 1991 at the National Championships. I don't think we said two words to each other in the race. The first time we hung out was before the Olympics in Barcelona. I had a pair of Ray-Ban sunglasses he liked, and he had a winter cycling jacket. I needed a jacket, so we did a trade.

We didn't have frequent contact, but we saw each other at some of the more important domestic races. Some years later I noticed a significant change in Lance's appearance. As we were waiting for the start of the Tour DuPont, I jokingly asked him if he was playing linebacker for the Dallas Cowboys — his arms were massive, and he had a barrel chest. I was pretty sure he was juiced up. He was huge, not fat, but lots of muscle and power. He won the overall and five stages that year. When I quit cycling in 1997, I never thought we would cross paths again; in fact, I figured he would be hard pressed to even remember who I was.

But we reconnected in June 2013. By then I was known to the cycling public as the Anti-Lance because of my refusal to dope. I'd just joined Twitter, and I was taken aback and even uncomfortable to see that I, someone who was well-known for my anti-drug stance, had the disgraced Lance Armstrong as one of my followers.

I wasn't sure what he wanted, and I sent him a quick message, saying: "Hey Lance, thanks for the follow ... if there's anything I can do for you, my cell phone is ..." His response was quick and cryptic: "You bet. We get to Aspen June 22 and there thru Sept. Let's catch up then. Lots to discuss."

Lots to discuss? What did he mean by that? I had some business in Aspen in late June, so we agreed to meet at his house on June 25. I don't get rattled easily, but I was nervous about this get-together. During the two-hour drive from my home in Grand Junction, I was undistracted by the Rocky Mountain scenery of late June: whitewater caps on the Colorado River and tourists stewing in natural hot springs. Instead, I could only guess at what this meeting was all about. *Was I walking into a trap?* I asked myself. I assumed this meeting would be slightly confrontational and that he would record our conversation.

During the drive up, he sent me a text: "Hey, did you bring your bike?"

"Sure," I texted back. And he responded, "Sweet, let's ride." That was encouraging because then I knew it was going to be a social meeting. We were both going to be in our comfort zone, riding bikes. We would be able to talk with no ringing phones, no kids, no business and best of all, no one eavesdropping.

When I got to his house, Lance immediately told me to use his bathroom to change into riding clothes.

He took my bike out of the car, put the front wheel on the bike, and filled up a water bottle. It was so familiar and so bizarre. I mean we hadn't seen each other in seventeen years, and we were never close. It was weird, really, to watch Lance Armstrong put my front wheel on, grab a water bottle, and pump my tires. I thought, *What the fuck? Lance is like an old buddy here!*

Lance shooed me with his hands and told me to hurry the fuck up. The f-bomb is a frequent part of his vocabulary, which it is of mine, too.

Then it was handshakes and small talk, like old buddies catching up — *How are the kids, your wife, your job?*

Eventually we threw our legs over our bikes and talked while we rode, heading toward the old silver-mining town of Ashcroft, 10 miles south of Aspen on Castle Creek Road. It's now a ghost town. It seemed appropriate that ghosts would be along for this ride.

The first thing Lance asked me about was Colorado Mesa University. Through Livestrong, he had sponsored a fundraiser for Butch Miller, the former athletic director and a cancer survivor. I was impressed, because Lance must have sponsored thousands of events for people, and yet he remembered Butch and the people who helped with the Livestrong event. I figured that to remember this he must have a memory like a steel trap.

We talked about his lifetime ban from competitive cycling and other endurance events. It had been nearly a year since the USADA report and his ban, but Lance's anger was still right below the skin.

He said the United States Anti-Doping Agency and its CEO, Travis Tygart, weren't fair to him. I pointed out that for the doping authorities, he was like the gangster Al Capone and Tygart was like persistent prohibition agent Eliot Ness. I didn't feel sorry for him. You reap what you sow.

I asked Lance how he was holding up and he told me it was stressful, but he still was better off than if he would have stayed in Plano, Texas.

Lance grew up poor; everyone knows his scrappy, boot-straps story. I grew up poor, too, and getting a degree from Cal gave me options other than riding a bike for a living, but there's no way I would have ruined people's lives the way Lance did to protect a lie. I'm just not wired that way. It takes a certain type of person to attack the truth the way he did.

He said that with my Berkeley degree I had to know I was going to be okay.

Eventually, I did. But being okay isn't the same as riding into Paris on the best team in the history of cycling. I paid a heavy price for my decision, a price few people can understand. The lost experiences and the money are only part of the equation. The biggest price was not realizing my full potential as a cyclist. I'll never know how good I really could have been.

At one point Lance asked me if I thought I could have won seven Tours if I had doped.

"Of course not," I answered. "But I certainly would have been in the mix. Tyler won a fucking gold medal, and Liege! Julich won Paris-Nice and podiumed at the Tour. Hincapie won a fucking mountain stage."

He looked at me and told me I was right.

Few people can understand the decisions Lance made like I can. Even though I made a different choice, it doesn't discount the fact that I know the choices he faced, and I know there were going to be consequences either way.

Lance is always big on saying to his critics: "You don't understand. You weren't there."

I was there. And I do understand. And that's what scared me so much. I had a hard decade when I quit racing. My family struggled for ten years financially and emotionally.

I let him lead the conversation. I didn't want to come out and say, "Why are we here?" He would get around to that. *Maybe he does need a friend,* I thought.

I wasn't sure I was the right guy for that. I remembered all the tell-all books from his former teammates, like Tyler and George. Who is different from them? Me.

Lance and the Anti-Lance going for a friendly bike ride. Even in the moment it felt surreal.

On Castle Creek Road we passed several other cyclists. One did a reflexive double-take at Lance. Most people know he lives nearby, but he still has celebrity star power when people see him in the flesh.

He asked about a mutual friend, Peter Stubenrauch. Lance wanted to know what Peter thought about his situation. I said that Peter and I were pretty much on the same page — we hated the lying and bullying, but we respected him as an athlete. After about an hour and twenty minutes we'd looped back to Lance's house.

For a while we continued to meet for an occasional road or mountain bike ride. We texted and spoke on the phone from time to time. In some ways I was like a fanboy, enamored with his attention to me. The truth is, I wanted to be his friend. In my hubris I thought maybe I could be a positive influence on him, to in some small way help him make ethical decisions. I saw what he wanted me to see. It's embarrassing, but probably true.

People have an opinion about Lance Armstrong, worldwide, whether they know him or not. Lance doped, cheated, lied, and covered it up, but you can't discount the good he has done either. I'm not saying it excuses his past behavior, but things need to be kept in context.

The magnitude of winning seven Tours de France in a row is astounding. Nothing went wrong, the team delivered, Lance didn't have a bad day, he didn't get sick. You think of 140, 150, or 160 days racing the Tour, and he never had a day that cost him the race, not one.

Doping may have been against the rules, but it was part of the sport. Nearly everyone was doing it.

It was difficult for me, watching Postal, my former team, win again and again knowing that I'd willingly walked away, that if I'd made a different decision I'd have been drilling it up the slopes of Alpe d'Huez to put my teammate in a position to win. On the one hand, I was proud that an American team, a team I had been part of, was kicking everyone's ass. On the other hand, I knew they were lying through their teeth. Their arrogance really grated on me. It made me so angry, this myth of Cancer Jesus and the Blue Train. They were doped to the gills and had the temerity to attack anyone who suggested otherwise. I got flashbacks of that with the way President Trump lied and the sycophants lined up to kiss his ass. It drove me crazy.

The irony, of course, is that people say, *Well, if everyone was doing it, then the results would have been the same anyways.* That's certainly what Lance believes. But the truth is, we don't know.

The drugs affect people differently. Some got a huge performance enhancement while others did not. It's important to remember that at this time in the sport there was no test for EPO. There was just an arbitrary hematocrit test of 50. If you were above 50 you tested positive, but if you were below 50 you were fine. So, someone with a natural hematocrit level in the high 40s was not going to get nearly the boost in performance someone in the low 40s would get.

It's impossible to say Lance would have won those Tours if everyone was clean. They weren't. And he did win. He won seven Tours de France in a row. That's what we know. That makes him a successful athlete, but it ends there.

Lance is not part of my life. We're not close. We're not friends and we're not enemies. Several years ago my family and I moved to the Aspen area. It's a small mountain community, and the cycling community is even smaller, so Lance and I would occasionally see each other on the trail, bike path, or just walking around town.

When the Lance Armstrong charade came crashing down following his disastrous Oprah Winfrey interview in January of 2013, it was the biggest sports story of the time. Lester Holt, then with the *Today* show, asked me in a televised interview if, despite it all, I thought Lance was worthy of redemption.

I said: "Redemption is the key thing to focus on. Everybody is worthy of redemption. I think it's what you do to earn that. Whether he does the right things to earn that is not really for me to say."

I'm not sure if Lance will ever get the redemption he so craves. In the annals of history he will be known as one of the greatest frauds in the history of sport. In my mind he is not a man of honor. I wanted to give him the benefit of the doubt and see for myself what type of person he is. He is wicked smart, fun, and engaging, but a man of character he is not.

The last time I rode with Lance, we talked about our lives and our families. My son, Marius, had recently had an episode where he was anxious, depressed, and suicidal. Lance heard this from a mutual acquaintance and asked if there was anything he could do to help. Marius was interested in film editing and coding, so I asked Lance if he would hire Marius as an intern during his Tour podcast. Lance asked what Marius could do and I said: "Anything. He can go on coffee runs, pick up people at the airport, sweep floors, edit film, whatever. Even if it's just a few hours, it'll be good for him. And he'll be a help to you guys, too." I asked Lance to pay Marius but said I'd reimburse him. I thought working on a set could help Marius' confidence. Lance thought about it and agreed. I thanked Lance and told him that I'd have Marius contact him directly for a time to meet.

When I got home from the ride, I told Marius he had a job working for Lance during his podcast. Marius was elated.

"Friday's your start date, I said, "but you'll need to touch base with Lance to find out what time to be there." I tested his work ethic. "If he wants you there at 6 a.m., what time do you need to be there?"

Marius passed the test. "5:50," he answered. Marius texted Lance that he was excited to be working with him on his podcast, told him he had a drivers' license, and said he'd do whatever was needed. I warned Marius that Lance was not great at answering texts and he'd most likely need to send a follow-up. Two days later, Marius texted again, thanking Lance for the opportunity and asking what time he needed to be at the Aspen studio.

Later that evening I get a text from Lance saying he'd spoken to the production crew and they felt they had everything covered, so he wasn't going to need Marius after all. My initial reaction is the way I feel to this day: *Are you fucking kidding me? This is your show. You can find something for him to do!* I didn't respond to his text and have never spoken to Lance again. I didn't know how to tell Marius. He was excited about this opportunity and had already told all his friends. After a fitful night's sleep, I went into Marius' room and delivered the news. Marius was disappointed but said: "It's okay, Dad. It doesn't bother me. What bothers me is that Lance didn't tell me directly, but it's okay."

And that pretty much sums up my opinion about Lance: He's a man who just cannot accept consequences. He didn't even want to face the consequence of giving a 16-year old boy bad news. Time and again he made the choice that benefitted him, regardless of how that decision affected others.

I know that I must sound bitter, and perhaps I am. Some will assert that Lance's transgressions only became too much to me when they finally directly affected me. That's fair criticism. But I know this, and so does Lance: You don't fuck with people's kids. Especially when they're vulnerable. Lie to me, use me, deceive me, whatever. I'm a grown-ass man and can deal with it. But don't fuck with my kids.

Lance is who we thought he was.

Lance never did get around to telling me what he wanted from our first meeting, but now I have a pretty good idea. I think he wanted me to help sanitize his past misdeeds, to be able to point to me, the Anti-Lance, and say, "See, even Scott thinks I won those Tours."

I walked away from professional cycling rather than live a lie, even though I wanted nothing more than to compete and to win. I look back on the Tours that USPS won with both pride and envy. I would love to have ridden into Paris with eight of my teammates knowing that we were part of history.

But, for me, the price was too steep. Lance will forever be known as a fraud. But Lance also won seven Tours. I didn't even compete in one.

We all need to accept the consequences of our decisions. The decisions Lance and I made were completely different, but they had one thing in common: They were both extreme.

Chapter 19
SPORT AS PROXY FOR LIFE

Sport is the ultimate meritocracy. Everything
you do is measurable.

Observing the mechanics of a peloton can teach you a lot about how to — and how not to — try and get ahead. Success isn't just about going as hard as you can, although there's a time for that.

The trick is knowing when to attack.

An attack is when you make an aggressive, flat-out move to pull ahead of the peloton. It's violent. You are going with everything you have, and you are fighting the full force of the peloton. The power of the peloton at the professional level is almost mythic. It takes on an organic force of its own, like a hell-bent dragon, yielding to no one.

In a peloton there are 150 to 200 professionals who are all highly skilled, trained, and prepared. The peloton's shape follows the laws of aerodynamics: a wedge, like geese flying in formation. It's a dynamic organism, skimming along the road surface. The riders at the front are doing 30 percent more work, and the riders in the middle have it easier; they can recover. But it's also dangerous in the middle because there are competitors in front of you, next to you, and behind you. You're surrounded. The peloton is like a swarm of angry bees, especially when the race is going fast.

191

Riders veer out from the outside, and then the peloton collapses in the middle. You can go from first position to the back of the peloton within a matter of thirty seconds if you are not vigilant and fighting the wheel to keep your position.

Inexperienced riders like to attack when it's easy, but that's the wrong time to attack because if it's easy for you it's easy for everybody. The time to attack is when you think you can't go, when it's really hard. That is what Brian Miller, my old Telluride coach, told me.

Brian was a professional cyclist in Telluride and one of the top pros in America for climbing. His directive always stuck with me, "When you are dying, and on the rivet and think you can't go anymore, you attack."

Everybody feels that way, that they are about to die. So you attack when everyone's dying, and then it's a mental game. You attack and go as hard as you can to get separation from the peloton. You don't want to attack from the front because everybody can see you and you don't have the element of surprise. You want to attack from fifteen or twenty riders back. By the time you hit the front, if the peloton is going 24 miles an hour, you are going 35 miles an hour and you get a gap.

Early on in my career when I was racing with the amateurs I was really strong — but I was really stupid, too. I would attack from the front, and it would work because I was so much stronger than anyone else. But brute strength alone doesn't work at the highest levels of sport. You have to use your head.

There is a controlled environment in the sporting world. There's a start, there's a finish, and there's a result. Success is defined in an absolute: winning or losing. It's the ultimate meritocracy. Everything you do is measurable. If you are a professional athlete you are measured by your results, and it's obvious if you're successful or not. And everyone wants your job. If you don't get the job done, there are plenty of people waiting for their shot. If you're a quarterback you've got to get the pass to the wide receiver. If you're a runner you've got to get to the finish line first. If you're a cyclist you've got to contribute to your team.

Cycling is a brutal sport that demands almost biblical levels of suffering. At times you sacrifice your own ambitions for the success of others. At other times, when you have been anointed as a team leader and your teammates are burying themselves for you, you can dig deeper to honor the sacrifice of others.

This type of commitment can translate to success in life. Business, academics, and relationships take a mixture of suffering and sacrifice to be successful. Success also requires give and take. There are times when the team is racing for you and there are times when you're racing for the team. The times when the team is racing for you, you find you can push harder than you thought possible, to respect that sacrifice the team is making for you. You don't want to let the team down.

The flip side of the coin is that sometimes you are the worker and you are sacrificing and suffering to put your team leader in a position to win.

In the same way you serve different roles on your team, you'll serve different roles in life, and those roles will change over time. As you go through various phases — when you find a spouse and maybe start a family — you know those things are almost always mutually exclusive from sport.

To be a pro cyclist, you are either training or recovering. It requires a sacrifice and a selfishness to get to the level of cycling where you can live in Europe and travel extensively, but then you don't have the time or the will to enjoy it. It is a Catch-22: You are in this great position, but it is also a horrible position because you have to be so focused on the task of winning that nothing else matters.

You can't consider other people's needs or wants, because if you do you are not doing everything you can do to become a professional athlete. So somebody who is wholly committed is going to take your job. They want it so they will do whatever they have to do.

It's difficult to be a great athlete and to also be a great spouse and a great dad. The single-minded focus that makes you a better athlete can take the focus away from where it's needed the most: being a supportive partner and a present dad. Maybe this is a wisdom that comes when you get a little older. When I was 20, I was more aggressive than I am now. I was a different person at 30 and 40 and even in my 50s today.

But, hopefully, you become more introspective and ask, *If I am a cog in the wheel, what is my role today?*

I can be a little bit more selfish today, now that my kids are older and more independent, than I could be when I had a 2-year-old and a 6-year-old. Their needs were a lot greater then. I don't know if I am completely successful as a father and a husband— we certainly had our hard times — but I tried to prioritize my family. It takes commitment to find balance and fully understand when it's time to take, when it's time to give, and also when it's time to compromise.

It's hard to do; it doesn't just happen. I think you consciously have to make an effort to keep perspective. If you look at your first three decades of life, that's a time to take — you should be taking and learning about yourself. But then there comes a point in your life when it's about giving. By then our decisions are based more on the needs of others than on the needs of ourselves.

If you want to be successful in your family, you have to give. The giving's much harder because you don't have control. You don't always know if you're giving what's needed. When you're taking, that's easy, because you can have much more effect on the outcome.

Sport is also a great teacher of resilience: When you fall down, you get up. If you watch a road race, cyclists crash a lot. It hurts when you hit the pavement at 25 miles an hour and skid across it: soft flesh on blacktop sandpaper.

You still get up and finish the race. You have to get back in the saddle — not just to overcome your fears, but because that is what is expected. It is no fun. Your shorts are torn up and you're bleeding and you have road rash and bruises, but you get back on the bike. The next day you are going to be really sore, but you can slowly start healing and you can ride through the pain.

Sometimes you just have to grit it out. Cycling is intensely painful, but that physical discomfort, the pain, is short-lived. If you can stomach the pain you will get through it and maybe you'll win or maybe you won't, but the pain will pass.

The first year my daughter ran middle school track, she quit during a 1-mile race — pulled up exhausted, nauseated, and demoralized. She complained that she was in pain and felt like she was going to throw up. But she wasn't sick or injured. I was livid. I didn't care if she was going to be first or last, but our family are not quitters.

I lit into her saying: "You should always finish a race, even if you are dead last. I don't care if you have to walk or crawl, but you finish the race!"

The next year, she made significant progress. She didn't win any races, but she ran a 6:25-minute mile, improving from an almost 9-minute mile from the previous year. I was psyched for her. She made a huge improvement to where she was competitive and finished in the top three or four every race. She was right up there until the end with the girls who would have lapped her the previous year.

Hard work and grit make all the difference. Yes, natural ability is a factor, but if you want something, you have to work for it.

Not that everything always goes according to plan. There are going to be times in life when you have a colicky kid or you're flat broke. There are going to be uncomfortable times in family relationships. Whenever you're faced with a setback or disappointment, you have to ask yourself if you're going to quit or if you're going to get back in the saddle and try to make it another day.

Discomfort is not something you avoid. It's something you go through to get to something better. Whether you can see it or not, success may be just on the other side of that rough patch.

And to win at anything in life, you have to take a risk. It's not easy. It's easier, in road racing, to stay in the pack and finish in the top twenty. But if you want to win you have to take a risk — go hard and suffer for it — and most of the time you are going to lose. If you win even one out of ten times from taking a risk, though, it's worth it.

Most of the time you are going to fail — even with the best preparation and the best strategy. You're judged on your results. If you want better results, whether in sports or in life, take the risks that will put you in a position to get them. If you look at successful entrepreneurs, for example, many of them have serially failed, but then they find that one thing that works and stick with it. They are not afraid to fail.

Success is relative. In softball, for instance, you are going to fail at the plate 70 percent of the time. You go into it with that expectation. But the other 30 percent is a full measure of success.

I was in a meeting once where the speaker talked about the fine line between good and great. He cited an example when Tiger Woods was No. 1 in the field, and the 100th golfer in the world was just two strokes difference. If you look at the Tour de France, the difference in time between first place and last is usually 4 percent or less.

Sport teaches you the linear relationship between the effort you put in and the result you get — even if it is something as basic as doing a push-up. If you ask a 12-year-old kid to do five push-ups, most could probably only do one or two. But if a 12-year-old starts working on push-ups three or four days a week, he or she may get up to five, then eight, then ten. Hard work will equal a result every time.

The harder you work, the closer you'll get to the limits of your natural abilities. When my son was in sixth-grade, the kids at swim class called him "Slow Fish." He didn't have a lot of success at school athletics. He said he was the last one picked on a team, and I can relate to that. When I was in school, when it came time for friends to pick teammates for dodge ball or anything else, I was the last kid picked, too. But I explained to him (when he could hear between his sobs) that he hadn't put in enough effort to be successful. If he wanted to be a faster swimmer or the kind of ringer kids wanted on their team, he was going to have to put the work into it.

On one hand I was sympathetic to his hurt feelings, but I also asked him what he wanted to do about the situation. Was he going to quit or was he going to work hard to overcome it? He decided he wanted to overcome it, so we worked at it. Three days a week he jumped rope and did push-ups and pull-ups. It made a difference in his confidence. I don't care whether he becomes a world-class athlete or not, but I want him to know that he can take steps to improve his situation in life — even if it's just swimming faster than a Slow Fish — and I also want him to be able to defend himself physically if he needs to.

Physical activity is part of my identity. Plus, I just feel better if I'm fit. I'm not interested in being an elite cyclist anymore. I love to ride, but to be an elite cyclist — even as a Masters — you don't have balance. You have to be so light that you're not necessarily going to have a strong core or even be able to do five pull-ups. You just can't carry the weight.

Now I'm trying to go for overall fitness where my bones get more density and my core is stronger. I'm mixing in riding my bike with skiing and weightlifting. Mandie and I ride our bikes together and we work out with weights once or twice a week. I always feel better after a workout, even though I might be sore. It goes back to balance. I don't want to spend so much time at my job that I neglect my health and my family. Maybe by finding balance I am more successful. Fitness is and always will be a part of my life.

I don't have all the answers, but I think it's a good exercise to ask yourself, when faced with an obvious shortcut, a cheat: *Will you be proud not only of your achievement, but also of how you won it?* Because how you win follows you for life.

That's my story. I wasn't the fastest, or the most celebrated, or the winningest cyclist. Ultimately, my real wins are not counted in trophies, or sponsorships, or adoration, but in being true to myself. Doing the right thing matters. How you win matters.

My hope is that my story can inspire the little guy to stand up for what is right, that people can see through my example that while making tough decisions may be painful, once you've made one tough decision, it becomes easier and easier to make another one. And then another one.

And then you're on a path you can be proud of. You're going to lose more often than you win, but when you do win, you win true.

ACKNOWLEDGMENTS

Writing a book is a team sport, too. The authors are grateful for the friends, family, and other supporters who helped bring this story to the page. Scott's mother, Susan Kees, encouraged him to explore and read and write. Bill Kees was the original inspiration for Scott's life in cycling; none of this would have been possible without his encouragement. Journalist Robin Dearing first suggested Scott's story to *The Grand Junction Daily Sentinel.* Publisher Jay Seaton recognized the book's potential, based on Scott's cycling columns written for the sports section. Early drafts of the book came together at 734 S. Seventh St. Graphic artist Robert García designed the cover and photo pages. Press technician Dan Bennett scanned and adjusted photographs for print quality. Peter Cossins, Piper Davis, Kunal Prakash, Rich Sale, and Pamela Shafer provided developmental editing suggestions and proofreading. Laurena's husband, Scott Davis, was unflaggingly supportive through the twists that publishing projects take. Mandie Mercier provided tireless reading and support throughout the book and throughout Scott's life.

Win True

ABOUT THE AUTHORS

Scott Mercier is first and foremost a husband, father, and friend. He works in finance, owns a small real estate company, is a public speaker, and writes a cycling column for Carmichael Training Systems. Scott was valedictorian of his class of thirteen from Telluride High School, earned a degree in Economics from U.C. Berkeley, is a Certified Financial Planner™, and is working on a master's in finance from the Harvard University Extension School. He was Telluride's first Olympian, representing Team USA in 1992 at the Barcelona Games. He competed as a professional cyclist from 1993 to 1997 and finished his career as a member of the infamous U.S. Postal Services Cycling Team. Scott lives in Basalt, Colorado, with Mandie, his wife of twenty-five years.

Laurena Mayne Davis is an award-winning journalist, editor, and writer. Laurena is a Ph.D. student in Technical Communication and Rhetoric at Texas Tech University and a graduate of Northern Arizona University and Colorado Mesa University (CMU). She is a lecturer in Communication Studies at CMU in western Colorado, where she lives with her husband, Scott Davis.

Win True

Made in the USA
Middletown, DE
05 May 2024

53880770R00126